THiNK

STUDENT'S BOOK 4B **B2**

Herbert Puchta, Jeff Stranks & Peter Lewis-Jones

CONTENTS

	FUNCTIONS & SPEAKING	GRAMMAR	VOCABULARY
Unit 5 **Screen time** p 48	Advice and obligation Talking about technology	Obligation, permission and prohibition (review) Necessity: *didn't need to / needn't have* Ability in the past (*could, was / were able to, managed to, succeeded in*)	Technology (nouns) Technology (verbs)
Unit 6 **Bringing people together** p 56	Using intensifying comparatives Discussing the use of the Internet for doing good Role play: Stuck in a lift	Comparatives Linkers of contrast	Ways of speaking Love and relationships

Review Units 5 & 6 pages 64–65

	FUNCTIONS & SPEAKING	GRAMMAR	VOCABULARY
Unit 7 **Always look on the bright side** p 66	Cheering someone up *Silver linings* game: – thinking of optimistic solutions	Ways of referring to the future (review) Future continuous Future perfect	Phrases to talk about the future: *about to, off to, on the point of* Feelings about future events **Wordwise:** Expressions with *so*
Unit 8 **Making lists** p 74	Saying 'Yes' and adding conditions Discussing wonders of the world	Conditionals (review) Mixed conditionals	Phrasal verbs (2) Alternatives to *if*: *suppose, provided, as long as, otherwise, unless*

Review Units 7 & 8 pages 82–83

Pronunciation pages 121 **Get it right!** pages 124–125
Speaking activities pages 127–128

PRONUNCIATION	THINK	SKILLS	
The schwa sound	**Train to Think:** The PMI strategy **Self-esteem:** Learning from elderly people	Reading	Texts: Smart screens? Article: Great success for teenage teachers: When silver surfers get connected Culture: When pictures learnt to walk and talk: the history of film
		Writing	Instructions
		Listening	A conversation about watching too much TV
Linked words with /dʒ/ and /tʃ/	**Train to Think:** Exaggeration **Values:** Doing good	Reading	Blog: The day people started talking Article: An Ice Cold Summer Literature: *A kind of loving* by Stan Barstow
		Writing	An essay about social media
		Listening	Radio show: *Radio romances*
Encouraging someone	**Train to Think:** Learning to see things from a different perspective **Self-esteem:** What cheers me up	Reading	Blog: Me, Myself and My take on the World Website page: QUOTATIONSforWORRIERS Photostory: The competition
		Writing	A short story ending: 'Every cloud has a silver lining'
		Listening	Radio show: *Silver Linings*
Weak forms with conditionals	**Train to Think:** The 'goal setting' checklist **Values:** Lists	Reading	Book review: *The Checklist Manifesto* by Atul Gawande Blog: Adrian's list blog Culture: The New Seven Wonders of the World
		Writing	An essay: A Modern Wonder of the World
		Listening	An interview about why we make lists

5 | SCREEN TIME

OBJECTIVES

FUNCTIONS: advice and obligation
GRAMMAR: obligation, permission and prohibition (review); necessity: *didn't need to / needn't have*; ability in the past (*could, was / were able to, managed to, succeeded in*)
VOCABULARY: technology (nouns); technology (verbs)

READING

1 How many different types of screen can you see in the photos? Can you think of other types of screen that you see or use in a typical day? Make a list.

2 Thinking of the list you made in Exercise 1, what are the advantages and disadvantages of having so many different screens in your daily life?

3 🔊 1.27 Read and listen to the texts and find out which of your ideas listed in Exercise 2 are mentioned.

4 Read the texts again. Match the paragraphs with the titles. There is one extra title.

- A The consequences of 24-hour availability — 3
- B It's a rich person's world — /
- C Parents need to establish limits — 1
- D Fewer screens, better lives — 2

5 Which text talks about …

a the harm screens can do even when we're not watching them?
b why none of us are really out of contact any more?
c the effect of screen time on the family?
d how it's almost impossible to live without modern technology?
e the financial implications of trying to limit the use of technology?
f the effects of spending too much time in front of a screen?

6 **SPEAKING** Work in pairs. Discuss the questions.

1 Think of a screen that your parents complain about you using too much. Why do they complain?
2 Think of one type of screen that you couldn't live without and one you could live without. Tell your partner and give reasons.

SMART SCREENS?

5 SCREEN TIME

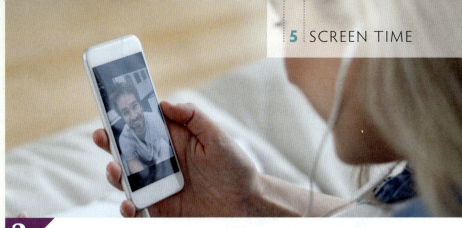

1 How much screen time do you allow your children? This has become one of the most challenging issues of modern parenting. Most experts are in agreement that screen time should be limited and warn against allowing children to spend too long in front of a screen. However, it's not always so easy to follow their advice. Clearly children can't see the potential harm that an excessive amount of time spent in front of a screen might do. Furthermore, peer pressure means that they feel unfairly disadvantaged when their parents say they must switch their electronic devices off, which in turn often leads to stressful family situations. It's easy to see why so many parents give in and let their children look at screens for far too long. Unfortunately this quick and simple solution creates greater problems in the long term, such as the negative effects on attention span, fitness levels and mood, as children become more and more irritable after being exposed to so much screen time. Of course, this is a situation that has been with us since the popularisation of TV in the 1960s; it's just with the predominance of screens in modern life, it's become a lot more serious.

2 Far from being dark at night, most modern cities are awash with colour from artificial lighting, and these huge TV screens and neon signs are making it difficult for many residents to get a good night's sleep. One city has decided to take action against this night time pollution.

With a population of over 11 million, São Paulo is the biggest city in Brazil and one of the ten biggest cities in the world. Not so long ago, the local government decided to pass the 'Clean City Law' which said that large outdoor advertising was not allowed any more and that all existing signs had to be taken down despite the financial losses it meant for the city. The advertising companies may not have been happy but the people living in the city were, with more than 70% agreeing that the ban had improved their quality of life.

3 Mobile phones have become such an important part of our lives that it's difficult to imagine how we could live without them. Of course, making and receiving calls is only one of their functions. We use them to take photos, record videos, check our email and Facebook accounts, surf the Internet, give us directions, play games, shop, check in for a flight, the list seems almost endless. But it wasn't all that long ago that people didn't need mobile phones and managed to live without them quite easily and maybe we were all just a little bit happier. In the old days, if you wanted to call someone, you phoned their house. If they weren't home, it was just bad luck. However, because the mobile phone is mobile, we now phone the person directly and if they don't pick up immediately then we get annoyed. We expect people to be reachable all day every day. The result of this expectation is that no one is allowed to relax any more. We're supposed to answer our phones whether we're at work, at home, on holiday or even asleep. We have lost the ability to be unreachable and to truly switch off.

TRAIN TO THINK

The PMI strategy

A good brainstorming strategy you can use when making decisions is the PMI strategy. On a piece of paper, draw three columns and head them 'plus', 'minus' and 'interesting'. Write down the positive consequences (plus) and negative consequences (minus) of taking the decision, and also what would be 'interesting' about carrying it out.

1 Look at the example below. Can you add any more ideas to the columns?

Books should be banned from schools

plus	minus	interesting
Lessons would be more interactive. Students wouldn't have to carry heavy books to and from school.	Students would spend even more time looking at screens.	How would this change teachers' lives?

2 **SPEAKING** Work in groups. Choose one of the situations. Use the PMI strategy to come to a decision.

- Your school has been asked to put on a play but you and your friends are not sure if you should take part as it will mean staying after school for the next six weeks.
- Your group has been asked to take part in a reality TV show. It involves living without any technology for a month. You are not sure whether you should take part.
- Your group has been invited to make a recommendation to the public transport service of your town as to whether mobile phones should be forbidden on buses, trains and trams.

GRAMMAR
Obligation, permission and prohibition (review)

1. **Complete the sentences from the texts on page 49. Then complete the rule with** *let, must, should, need to* **and** *not be allowed to*.

   1. Most experts are in agreement that screen time _should_ be limited.
   2. They feel unfairly disadvantaged when their parents say they _must_ switch their electronic devices off.
   3. Many parents give in and _let_ their children look at screens all the time.

   RULE: To express obligation or necessity, we can use *have to* or ¹_must_ (as in sentence 2).
   To say something is (or isn't) a good idea, we can use ²_should_ (as in sentence 1).
   To express no obligation or necessity, we can use *don't have to* or *don't* ³_need to_
   To express permission, we can use ⁴_let_ (as in sentence 3) and to say that something is not permitted we use ⁵_not allowed to_

   LOOK!
   - *had better* = something is a good idea and is often used as a warning. The form is always *had better* + base form of verb, even when talking about the present.
   - *be supposed to* = there's an obligation to do something but in reality people don't always do it. It is always used in the passive form (like *be allowed to*)

2. **Complete the second sentence so that it has a similar meaning to the first sentence. Use the word given. You must use between two and five words including the word given.**

   1. Their daughter can't go out after 8 pm. (allowed)
      Their daughter _____ go out after 8 pm.
   2. Our teacher expects us to put up our hand if we want to ask a question. (supposed)
      We _____ put up our hand if we want to ask a question.
   3. Their young son isn't allowed to watch TV all day. (let)
      They _____ their young son watch TV all day.
   4. You should really turn off the TV if you don't want to get a headache. (better)
      You _____ off the TV if you don't want to get a headache.

   Workbook page 46

FUNCTIONS
Advice and obligation

1. Imagine an exchange student is coming to your school for a few weeks. Write down three rules and three pieces of advice to help them.

   You have to arrive at school by 9 am.

2. **SPEAKING** Compare your sentences in pairs.

VOCABULARY
Technology (nouns)

1. **Match the words with the pictures.**
   1 USB port | 2 headset | 3 adaptor | 4 webcam
   5 plug | 6 charger | 7 'at' symbol | 8 power lead
   9 protective case | 10 wireless router

2. **Complete the sentences using the words in Exercise 1.**
   1. There's something wrong with that email address. There's no _____ in it.
   2. I forgot to bring a UK _____ so I couldn't plug in my laptop.
   3. I left the _____ for my phone at home and I'm almost out of battery. Can I borrow yours?
   4. You can't get a wifi signal? Have you checked if the _____ is switched on?
   5. My laptop's only got one _____ so I can't plug in my mouse and my phone at the same time.
   6. I couldn't use my laptop. I left the _____ at home and it was out of battery.
   7. I'm going to plug in my _____. I don't want everyone to hear what you're saying.
   8. It's the wrong _____. You need an adaptor.

   Workbook page 48

50

5 SCREEN TIME

LISTENING

1 **SPEAKING** Mark the statements with 1 (agree), 2 (depends) or 3 (disagree). Then compare your findings in class.

Watching TV …
1. can damage your brain.
2. is bad for your education.
3. is addictive.
4. is expensive.
5. is not as satisfying as spending time with friends.

2 🔊 1.28 Listen to the conversation. Which of the statements in Exercise 1 does Sheena mention?

3 🔊 1.28 Listen again. Complete the sentences.
1. Sheena wants to know why Aaron missed _____ on Saturday.
2. Aaron's been spending a lot of time _____ on his tablet recently.
3. Aaron asks Sheena if she thinks he's becoming a _____ .
4. Aaron's been staying up until _____ recently.
5. Sheena warns Aaron about hidden advertising or _____ placement in films.
6. Aaron wants to invite Sheena to an outdoor _____ on Sunday.

GRAMMAR

Necessity: *didn't need to / needn't have*

1 Look at the examples from the listening and answer the questions. Then complete the rule with *didn't need to do / needn't have done*.

I didn't need to go [to the stadium] because I was able to watch it live online.
You needn't have [bought two tickets] because I did …

1. Did Aaron go to the stadium?
2. Did Aaron buy two tickets?

> **RULE:** When we use ¹_____ (*needn't have done*), it means that someone did something but in fact it wasn't necessary.
> When we use ²_____ (*didn't need to*), it often means that someone didn't do something because it wasn't necessary.

2 Choose a or b to follow each of the sentences 1–6. You must use all of the sentences.

1. Mum cooked a big meal for us but we'd already eaten.
2. Mum came and ate with us at the restaurant.
   a. She needn't have cooked. **1**
   b. She didn't need to cook. 2
3. I spent ages doing my homework last night and now Mr Peters isn't here to take it in.
4. Mr Peters told us we had a choice to do the homework or not.
   a. I didn't need to do it. 4
   b. I needn't have done it. 3
5. She took her umbrella but it was a really sunny day.
6. The forecast said that it was going to be a lovely sunny day. So she left her umbrella at home.
   a. She didn't need to take it. 6
   b. She needn't have taken it. 5

▶ Workbook page 47

VOCABULARY

Technology (verbs)

Rewrite the sentences below, replacing the words in italics with the phrases in the list in the correct form.

to upgrade (your system) | to save (a document) | to browse the Internet | to plug (a laptop) in | to sync devices | to post an update | to stream (a video) | to connect to wifi

1. Jack's *watching* yesterday's match *on the Internet without downloading* it.
2. I can't *access the Internet without using a cable*. There's no signal here.
3. I'm a bit bored so I'm *looking at various websites on the Internet*.
4. I think you should spend some money *on improving your operating system*; it's very old.
5. You should always *make sure different devices (laptop, tablet, etc.) contain the same information* so you've always got a backup.
6. The printer's not working. Oh! It's not *connected to the electricity supply*.
7. Mia hasn't *added new content to her blog* on Facebook for a week. I hope she's OK.
8. Sam is always losing files because he often forgets to *store information on an electronic device*.

▶ Workbook page 48

SPEAKING

Discuss in pairs.
1. How often do you post updates on social media?
2. Which devices do you sync?
3. What was the last TV programme you streamed?

> **Pronunciation**
> The schwa sound
> Go to page 120. 🔊

51

READING

1 Look at the photo and answer the questions.
   1 What do you think the relationship between the people is?
   2 What do you think they are doing?

2 Read through the article quickly and check your answers.

3 Read again. Find examples in the article of how elderly people used technology.

Great success for teenage teachers: When silver surfers get connected

A new documentary called *Silver Surfers* shows the inspiring story of a group of teens helping elderly people to improve the quality of their lives by teaching them how to make use of the Internet. The people were aged between 76 and 93.

Rosemary Raynes, the director of the documentary, got the idea for the film when talking to her sisters Poppy and Amy about a project they had started several years before in Kingston, Canada. The two teenagers and a group of friends had a clear goal: they wanted to help elderly people to feel more connected to other people, through the use of the Internet.

They started the project after witnessing how the Internet had changed their own grandparents' lives. Their grandparents could use the Internet at a basic level but wanted to become more proficient. After the two girls had given them a few basic IT lessons, they were able to use the computer confidently, and became enthusiastic users of Skype, Facebook and email.

The two students were so motivated by that success that they got several of their friends to join them. Together, they started to visit a local home for elderly people. Many of the people there couldn't even switch on a computer without help. But the young people were amazed how much they had learned after only a few lessons.

It's fascinating to see how the silver surfers featured in the film all had very different interests. Some of them wanted to use Facebook to stay in touch with family members who had emigrated to countries as far away as Australia. Others were keen to get ideas for travelling, learning how to play an instrument or cooking.

The outcomes of the project were amazing: 89-year-old Sheila, together with a friend, managed to create a YouTube cooking tutorial; 93-year-old Marilyn succeeded in making a rap video; Albert, 89, initially wanted to learn how to use the web to find friends he fought with in World War II and in doing so he was struck by how easy it was to reconnect online with people he hadn't seen in decades. He even managed to use his newly acquired skills to reunite with his daughter who he had lost touch with.

The documentary has been met with great enthusiasm in several countries, and a number of follow-up projects have been launched. They are all aimed at helping elderly people to explore the benefits of technology, have fun, and stay in touch with others – thanks to a wonderful initiative by two teenage girls.

4 Read again and answer the questions.
   1 What is *Silver Surfers*?
   2 What does it show?
   3 Who started the project?
   4 What inspired them to start the project?
   5 Who did they get to join them?
   6 Where did they start giving lessons?
   7 What were some of the elderly people's interests?
   8 What were some of their achievements?

5 **SPEAKING** Discuss with a partner.
   1 What do you think of the Silver Surfer project?
   2 Would you be prepared to join such a project? Why (not)?
   3 Which example of the seniors' achievements impresses you the most?
   4 Have you ever tried to help someone you know with technology? Did you manage to teach them successfully?

5 SCREEN TIME

GRAMMAR

Ability in the past: could, was / were able to, managed to, succeeded in

1 Read the examples from the article and then complete the rule with *managed*, *succeeded*, *could*, *couldn't*.

1 Many of the people there **couldn't** even switch on a computer without help.
2 After [...] a few basic IT lessons, they **were able to** use the computer confidently.
3 The outcomes of the project were amazing: 89-year-old Sheila [...] **managed to** create a YouTube cooking tutorial.
4 93-year-old Marilyn **succeeded in** making a rap video.

> **RULE:** To talk about ability generally in the past we use ^{1}_____ / couldn't.
>
> To talk about ability at specific moments in the past, we use was / were able to (^{2}_____ to + infinitive, or ^{3}_____ in + gerund).
>
> To talk about a lack of ability at specific moments in the past, we use ^{4}_____ / wasn't (weren't) able to.

2 Choose the correct answer to complete the sentences.

1 She broke her mobile phone a week ago. She _____ to access any social networks since then.
   A couldn't   B hasn't been able   C hasn't succeeded
2 He was so moved by the award he received that he _____ continue with his speech.
   A wasn't able to   B succeeded in   C could
3 He played football again for the first time after his injury, but he only _____ play for 20 minutes.
   A could   B managed to   C succeeded in
4 She had to ask several people until she finally _____ in finding some help.
   A managed   B succeeded   C could
5 My little brother _____ to walk just before his first birthday.
   A could   B was able   C succeeded
6 I tried to climb that mountain once, but I _____ to get to the top because of the bad weather.
   A couldn't   B didn't succeed   C didn't manage

> Workbook page 47

THiNK SELF-ESTEEM

Learning from elderly people

1 You're going to talk about an elderly person who has qualities that you admire. Make notes on why you admire this person.

2 Which of the qualities you have noted do you think you would like to have in your own life?

3 What could you do to develop those qualities?

4 **SPEAKING** Discuss your ideas with your partner.

5 **WRITING** Write a paragraph that summarises what it is you have learnt by thinking about the person.

One of our neighbours is a man called Mr Carter. He is over 80 years old, but in many ways he seems to be very young. He's got an excellent sense of humour, and I've had great conversations with him. He's a very good listener, and asks very interesting questions. If there is one thing I would like to learn from him for my own life then it is the way he seems to set goals for himself and goes for them. For example, Mr Carter has a little swimming pool in his garden, and he goes for a swim every day, no matter what the weather is. And the weather can be quite cold at times where we live!

Culture

1 **SPEAKING** Discuss the questions in pairs.
   1 Have you ever seen a silent film?
   2 Have you ever seen a film in black and white?

2 Scan the text to find the answers to these questions.
   1 What technology did Etienne Gaspar Robert use to impress his audiences?
   2 What did Edison and Dickenson invent and how did it work?
   3 What years are referred to as the 'Golden Era of Hollywood'?

3 🔊 1.31 Read and listen and check your answers to Exercise 2.

When Pictures Learnt to Walk and Talk: The History of Film

Early days: the magic lantern

Since its early days, the evolution of the art of film has been influenced by the development of science.

Several scientists in the 18th century (amongst them Kircher, Huygens and Fontana) developed devices that used hand-drawn pictures on a reflecting surface, a candle and a simple lens to project images onto a wall. These devices are what are now referred to as 'magic lanterns'.

More than a hundred years later, in 1798 in Paris, Etienne Gaspar Robert's magic lantern presentations were the talk of the town. His audience sat on one side of a transparent screen while he sat on the other with his magic lantern. He regularly succeeded in scaring his enthusiastic audiences with images of witches, ghosts and other spooky creatures. He created these images by using various technical tricks such as moving the lantern, using a shutter to create fading effects and changing the focus. In many ways, his shows were the forerunner of modern horror films.

The invention of film

The late 19th century saw the development of reel film. At first it was made of paper and then, later, of a scientific invention called celluloid. In the USA, Thomas Edison and William Dickenson invented a camera that automatically took a picture of a moving object every half second. The pictures were then transferred onto film and could be watched through a machine called the kinetoscope. The film could only be watched by one person at a time, looking through a small window to see the moving images.

The next step in the evolution of film was when brothers Auguste and Louis Lumière developed the cinematographe, which made it possible to take moving pictures and project large images. This used the same lens technology as that which had been developed for the magic lantern. They started producing short films that were all roughly 50 seconds long. The most famous one was *The Arrival of a Train at La Ciotat Station*. It is said that when the film was shown for the first time, the audience was so startled by the huge image of the train coming towards them that they started to scream and run away.

Hollywood

The 1920s were the most important years for the development of modern film. In that period, film studios came into existence and 'stars' were born. The film industry began to flourish, with Hollywood becoming the world's number one place for film production, with over 800 films being made there each year.

The 1930s are often called the Golden Era of Hollywood, which is famous for the development of the first talkies (up to then all films had been silent), documentaries and also Western films.

These days, of course, modern cinema audiences are used to state-of-the-art computer generated imagery (CGI) to bring fantastical worlds and unbelievably realistic creatures onto the screen in stunning 3D. It's sometimes difficult to see how it can be improved upon. But as science and technology continue to develop at lightning speed, we can assume that our cinematic experience will continue to get better and better.

4 Answer the questions.
   1 What did the first magic lanterns consist of?
   2 How did Etienne Gaspar Robert scare his audiences?
   3 What was the limitation of the kinetoscope?
   4 How did the Lumière brothers impress their spectators?
   5 Why did Hollywood become so famous?

5 SCREEN TIME

5 **VOCABULARY** Match the highlighted words in the article with the definitions.

1 very surprised
2 a round, wheel-shaped object on which film, etc. can be rolled
3 scary
4 a curved piece of glass in a camera or projector that makes objects seem closer, larger, smaller, etc.
5 something that acted as an early less advanced model of another thing that will appear in the future
6 that you can see through
7 the part of a reel film projector that opens to allow light to reach the film
8 grow rapidly

SPEAKING

Work with a partner. Discuss the questions.

1 Why don't some people like films with special effects?
2 Make a list of films with great special effects.
3 What's your favourite 3D film? Why?
4 What do you think will be the next stage in the development of film?

WRITING

Instructions

1 Read the instructions on how to save a Word file. Who do you think it has been written for and why?

2 Complete with the missing words. Then check in the instructions.

1 _____ your file is a written document, _____ you will be using a word processing program.
2 The _____ _____ you need to do is to create a new file.
3 _____ _____ this, open up the program.
4 _____ save the file, click on 'file' again.
5 _____ _____ you will be able to find your file easily.
6 _____, when you close your document, a dialogue box will appear.

3 Use a word or phrase from the list to complete each sentence.

this means | then | To | If | Finally | first thing

1 To take photos, the _____ you need is a camera.
2 _____ you're serious about photography, _____ buy the best camera you can afford.
3 Choose a camera with a high number of pixels – _____ that you'll have good quality images.
4 _____ find out which are the best cameras, do research on the Internet.
5 _____, start snapping and have fun!

One of the most important things you need to learn to do when using a computer to write documents is to learn how to save a file.

1 If your file is a written document, then you will be using a word processing program such as Microsoft Word. The first thing you need to do is to create a new file. To do this, open up the program by clicking on the icon.

2 When the program has opened, click on the icon 'file' in the top left hand corner of the screen and choose 'new' from the drop down menu. This will create a new document for you.

3 I would recommend saving this document, before you have written anything. This means that if your computer shuts down unexpectedly, you won't lose the file. To save the file, click on 'file' again. From the drop down menu choose 'save'.

4 A dialogue box or window will open asking you to type in the name of your document. You will also need to choose a location for the file. Select 'desktop' from the list on the left hand side of the box. This means you will be able to find your file easily when you start your computer.

5 Finally, when you close your document, a dialogue box will appear asking if you want to save any changes. Click 'yes' and this will ensure you never lose any of your work.

4 **SPEAKING** Discuss why the following tips are important when writing instructions.

Tips for writing instructions.
- Think carefully about who you are writing for.
- Use clear language that is easy to understand.
- Give the instructions in a logical order.
- Use a friendly, informal style.

5 Choose one of the computing processes below and write down short notes for each stage.

- how to create a folder
- how to change the font
- how to cut and paste
- how to rename a file

6 Write a text (120–180 words) describing the process you chose in Exercise 5. Remember to:

- decide who you are writing these instructions for (a child? a beginner? a fairly experienced user?).
- give your instructions in a logical order.
- think about the tips in Exercise 4.

55

6 BRINGING PEOPLE TOGETHER

OBJECTIVES

FUNCTIONS: using intensifying comparatives
GRAMMAR: comparatives; linkers of contrast
VOCABULARY: ways of speaking; love and relationships

READING

1 **SPEAKING** Work in pairs. Look at the photos. Describe the situations and how the people might be feeling, using these adjectives.

packed | stuffy | impatient | dull | polite | excited

> *The train is packed and some people haven't got anywhere to sit.*

2 **SPEAKING** Choose one of the people and imagine their thoughts. Make notes. Tell your partner the person's thoughts for your partner to guess who it is.

3 🔊 1.32 Look at the title. What do you think happened? Why did people start talking and why might the writer have thought this was a good thing? Read and listen to the blog, to check your ideas.

4 Read the blog again. Answer the questions.
 1 How long, usually, is the writer's train journey?
 2 After the second announcement, what was the first thing people started to talk about?
 3 What did the writer find out about other people?
 4 In what way(s) did people help each other?
 5 Why was the nurse 'welcomed as a hero'?
 6 What did people do when the train started moving?
 7 What was the train journey like the next day?

5 **SPEAKING** Work in pairs and discuss the questions.
 1 Would this be different if it happened in your country, do you think? If so, how?
 2 What other situations can you think of in which strangers might start talking to each other?
 3 Can you remember a time when you started a conversation with someone you didn't know and realised that your first impressions were wrong?

Stuck in a lift

ROLE PLAY Work in groups of four. Students A and C: Go to page 127. Students B and D: go to page 128.
Imagine you are four strangers travelling together in a lift. Suddenly the lift breaks down. An engineer has been called but won't be there for half an hour. Agree together on what you should do.

6 BRINGING PEOPLE TOGETHER

The day people started TALKING

My journey home from school is nothing special. The train's always busy but I usually find a seat and start reading or texting my friends, making sure, like everyone else, not to look at other people. Then, twenty minutes later, I get off.

But last Tuesday was different. I was happily looking out of the window listening to some new music I'd downloaded that morning when the train suddenly stopped. This wasn't unusual and I didn't think anything of it. Then after about five minutes, I noticed people were starting to get a bit annoyed. They were looking around and tutting to themselves. Fifteen minutes later, people started getting more and more annoyed – the train still hadn't moved. The longer the train stood still, the more annoyed people became until finally the dreaded announcement came: 'We are sorry to announce that this train is delayed.'

That seemed to calm people down and so we all went back to what we were doing before, but soon there was another announcement: we were going to be there for a long time – a train had broken down in front of us. There was a loud groan throughout the carriage but then something unexpected happened: complete strangers started talking to each other. At first, everyone just complained about the trains, but then people started talking about real things. I started chatting to a couple of young tourists sitting opposite me. They were from Spain and they were travelling around the UK so I recommended some places they should visit. They were having an amazing time and were taking the delay in their stride. Next, I really surprised myself by starting a conversation with a businesswoman. It turned out that there was so much more to her than a suit. She spends her weekends mountain-climbing and was going to take three months off work to climb Everest. It was fascinating talking to her. I've been wrong all my life, business people are a lot cooler than I thought. Then I decided to get up and go for a walk down the train. I met a woman who had been a student at my school seven years before and knew lots of my teachers. It seems my teachers were just as strict then as they are now.

People offered each other food and drink. A young woman took out her guitar and soon we were singing along. It was so much fun. While we were singing, we heard there was a diabetic man in another part of the train who needed help, and the woman from my school jumped into action. It turned out she was a nurse, and when she came back she was welcomed as a hero.

Then, after two and a half hours, we started moving again. Everyone clapped and cheered and some people, complete strangers three hours before, even hugged.

Of course, this journey didn't change anything. I took the train again on Wednesday but none of my new 'friends' were there. All the faces were new. Although people were polite, they weren't nearly as friendly as the people the day before had been. So I sat down and started texting. But I'll never forget the day the train stopped and people started talking.

TRAIN TO THINK

Exaggeration

When we feel emotional about something, we tend to exaggerate – we call something 'a brilliant idea', 'the best (film) ever', 'an amazing journey', etc. But we often don't mean that literally. As a listener you need to be aware of exaggeration and understand what the speaker is really saying.

1 Read the example and answer the questions.

> Last night's train journey was terrible. It was the worst journey of my life. The train was two hours late and then it stopped for ages in the middle of nowhere. I was so bored I thought I was going to go mad. I hope today's journey won't be so bad.

1 How many exaggerations does the speaker make?
2 What are they?
3 What does he really mean in each case?

2 **SPEAKING** Work with a partner. Tell them about something really good or bad that happened to you recently. Use exaggeration.

Pronunciation

Linking words with /dʒ/ and /tʃ/
Go to page 120.

GRAMMAR
Comparatives

1 **Match the sentence halves from the blog. Then read the rule and complete it with 1–5.**

1 The longer the train stood still,
2 Business people are a lot
3 It seems my teachers were just as
4 Although people were polite, they weren't nearly as
5 People started getting more

a friendly as the people the day before had been.
b and more annoyed.
c the more annoyed people became.
d cooler than I'd thought.
e strict then as they are now.

RULE:

A Use *a lot / far / much* + comparative to make a comparative stronger. **Sentence** 2

B Use *just as*, *not nearly as* and *nowhere near as* + adjective + *as* to intensify a comparison. **Sentences** 3 and 4

C Use comparative *and* comparative + short adjectives e.g. *hotter and hotter* to talk about how something or someone is changing or increasing. Use *more and more* + longer adjectives e.g. *more and more interesting*. **Sentence** 5

D Use *the* + comparative, *the* + comparative with short adjectives or *the more* + adjective, *the more* + adjective + clause with long adjectives to show how two events affect each other. **Sentence** 1

2 **Complete the second sentence so that it has a similar meaning to the first sentence using the word given. You must use between two and five words, including the word given.**

1 Today's test was much easier than yesterday's test. (nowhere)
   Today's test was _____ as yesterday's test.
2 I'm practising the piano a lot and I'm getting much better. (practise)
   The more I _____ I get at playing the piano.
3 I'm sure the price of food is going up each month. (and)
   Food is getting _____ each month.
4 I've been seeing a lot of John recently and I'm beginning not to like him so much. (less)
   The more I see John, _____ I like him.

▶ Workbook page 54

FUNCTIONS
Using intensifying comparatives

1 **Look at what the writer recommended to the tourists. Match the three parts.**

1 You should visit Bath.	a *It's easily the best* time to visit.	i And *it's a whole lot cheaper* than the train.
2 You should travel around by bus.	b *It's far and away* the most beautiful city in the UK.	ii And *it's miles less* crowded than London.
3 You should come back in August.	c It's the easiest way to travel *by far*.	iii And *it's even warmer* than it is now.

2 **Make recommendations to visitors to your country using the sentences in Exercise 1 to help you. Then compare with a partner.**

You should go by Tube. It's easily the best way to travel and it's a lot quicker than walking.

VOCABULARY
Ways of speaking

1 **Which one of these sentences was probably *not* said on the train in the blog on page 57?**

1 'Do you know what's wrong with the train?'
2 'You should definitely visit Manchester.'
3 'There's never anywhere to sit on these trains.'
4 'Hi, my name is Raffa and this is Clara.'
5 'We're sorry to say the train has a problem.'
6 'It was me. I had the last piece of chocolate cake.'

2 **Match the sentences in Exercise 1 with the speaker's communicative aim in each one.**

☐ to recommend   ☐ to confess
☐ to introduce   ☐ to enquire
☐ to announce   ☐ to complain

3 **Use suffixes from the list to complete the table.**

-ation | -ion | -tion | -y | -ment | -t

1 to recommend	to make a *recommendation*
2 to confess	to make a _____
3 to introduce	to make an _____
4 to enquire	to make an _____
5 to announce	to make an _____
6 to complain	to make a _____

4 **Write an example for three of the functions above. Read them to your partner to guess.**

This is Jo.   *You're making an introduction.*

▶ Workbook page 56

6 BRINGING PEOPLE TOGETHER

LISTENING

1 Put the pictures in order to make a story about Sophie and Rob. Compare with a partner.

2 🔊 1.35 Listen to the story on a radio programme. Check your ideas in Exercise 1.

3 🔊 1.35 Listen again and complete the sentences.
1 Sophie had everything she wanted in her life apart from _____ .
2 The first time Sophie saw 'Train Man' they were on the _____ waiting for the train.
3 Sophie told all her _____ about 'Train Man'.
4 Sophie finally made contact with 'Train Man' by giving him a _____ .
5 She learned his name was Rob when he sent her an _____ .
6 Sophie was disappointed to find out that Rob had a _____ .
7 Rob sent Sophie a second email a _____ after he sent the first one.
8 Rob and Sophie _____ and then got married a year later.

VOCABULARY
Love and relationships

1 Complete the phrases from the story with the missing verbs.

get | split | ask | get | fall | start | go | go | get

1 to _____ in love (with someone) – to develop very strong feelings for someone
2 to _____ up (with someone) – to end a relationship
3 to _____ married (to someone) – to become husband and wife
4 to _____ engaged (to someone) – to agree to get married
5 to _____ (someone) out – to invite someone to do something (with romance in mind!)
6 to _____ out (together / with someone) – to become boyfriend and girlfriend
7 to _____ on a date (with someone) – to do something together (to see if you like each other)
8 to _____ a family – to have a child
9 to _____ over (someone) – to not be sad anymore about an ex

2 Use the phrases in Exercise 1 in the correct tense to complete the story of Sophie and Rob.

Rob finally [1]_____ with his girlfriend. When he had [2]_____ her, he asked Sophie out in an email. She was really happy and they [3]_____ a few days later. They got on really well and started [4]_____ with each other. They quickly [5]_____. On holiday in Australia, Rob asked Sophie to marry him. She said 'yes' and they [6]_____. The following year they [7]_____. Soon after they decided to [8]_____ and had a baby girl called Megan.

3 **SPEAKING** Work in pairs. Think of a famous couple. Tell their story to another pair using the phrases above.

▶ Workbook page 56

59

READING

1 Look at the photo and answer the questions.

1. What are the people doing?
2. Why do you think they are doing it?

2 Read the article and check your ideas. Explain the play on words in the last sentence.

3 Read the article again and mark the sentences T (true), F (false) or DS (doesn't say).

1. Pete Frates wanted to play professional baseball.
2. He was diagnosed with an illness called ALS in 2014.
3. If you did the Ice Bucket Challenge you didn't have to pay any money.
4. You had to film yourself doing the challenge.
5. Barack Obama refused to give any money to the charity.
6. Some people felt the Ice Bucket Challenge was a bit dangerous.
7. Nearly 10% of the UK population donated money through the Ice Bucket Challenge.
8. Some people thought it gave the wrong message about water.

SPEAKING

Work in pairs and discuss the questions.

1. Do you remember the Ice Bucket Challenge? Did you, or anyone you know, take part in it?
2. Do you think it was a good idea? Why (not)?
3. What would you have said to someone who refused to take part?
4. What other examples can you think of where people have used social media to raise money for charity?

An Ice Cold Summer

In the summer of 2014, a weird and wonderful craze swept across the world. Everywhere you looked people were pouring buckets of freezing water over their heads. The craze soon had a name – 'The Ice Bucket Challenge' and the idea behind it was to raise money for charity. Despite the popularity of the challenge, not many people knew where it had come from. In fact it was the idea of an American called Pete Frates. He had been a promising college baseball player who seemed to have a bright future with the Boston Red Sox. However, his career was cut short when he fell ill with a disease called amyotrophic lateral sclerosis (or ALS for short). ALS attacks the nervous system and can cause speech problems and paralysis. It can also kill. Frates wanted to do something to raise both money and awareness to help sufferers of ALS. He had a simple but brilliant idea.

The idea was that you chose a couple of friends and challenged them to pour a bucket of freezing water over their heads. If they did this then they paid $10 to the charity. If they refused, they paid $100. To prove they had done it, they had 24 hours to post a video of their challenge online. Then it was their turn to nominate two more people and challenge them.

Soon it had gone viral with plenty of celebrities worldwide joining in including Usain Bolt, Lady Gaga, Oprah Winfrey, Taylor Swift, Cristiano Ronaldo and even former US president George W. Bush. The US President Barack Obama and UK Prime Minister David Cameron were also challenged although they both refused to do it and donated the $100 instead. All in all, more than 2,500,000 videos were posted on Facebook from around 150 different countries. Many millions of pounds were donated to the charity.

However, not everyone viewed the Ice Bucket Challenge in such a positive light. Many people felt that it put too much pressure on people who did not want (or maybe could not afford) to support the charity. If you were chosen by a friend and decided you did not want to take part, you were seen as being mean and not entering into the fun. It was also later found that many people who did the challenge didn't actually make any donation at all. One study found that even though over 15% of the British population had done the challenge, only 10% of participants had actually given any money to charity. Other people pointed out that water is a valuable human resource that is in short supply for millions of people around the world. They criticised the challenge for being wasteful of water.

So was the Ice Bucket Challenge a good thing or not? That will always depend on who you talk to.

Nevertheless, for a few hot months of summer back in 2014 the Ice Bucket Challenge brought millions of people from all over the planet together for a 'cool' cause.

6 BRINGING PEOPLE TOGETHER

GRAMMAR
Linkers of contrast

1 **Read the example sentences about the article and use them to complete the rule.**

1. Most people thought the Ice Bucket Challenge was brilliant. **However**, there were people who disagreed.
2. **Despite** its popularity, many people didn't know where the idea had come from.
3. Pete Frates found the time to raise money for charity **in spite of** being quite ill.
4. **Although** he was challenged, Barack Obama decided not to pour water over his head.
5. I didn't do the challenge **even though** four of my friends nominated me.
6. Many people did the challenge without donating. **Nevertheless**, the charity still made a lot of money.

> **RULE:** To contrast ideas and facts, we use these linking words: *although, even though, however, despite, in spite of* and *nevertheless*.
> 1. *Despite* and _____ are followed by a noun phrase or a gerund. They can be used at the beginning or in the middle of a sentence.
> 2. *Although* and _____ are followed by a full clause. They can be used at the beginning or in the middle of a sentence.
> 3. *However* and _____ introduce the contrasting idea and come at the beginning of a new sentence. They are followed by a comma.

2 **Rewrite the sentences using the word in brackets.**

0. I didn't know anyone at the party but I still had a good time. (in spite of)
   In spite of not knowing anyone at the party, I still had a good time.
1. I studied hard for the test. I failed it. (despite)
2. He doesn't earn a lot of money. He gives a lot of it to charity. (However)
3. I'd seen the film before. I still really enjoyed it. (although)
4. I started to eat less. I didn't lose any weight. (in spite of)
5. It wasn't very warm. We had a good time at the beach. (Nevertheless)
6. I don't speak a word of Chinese. I understood what he said. (even though)

3 **Rewrite this idea using each of the linkers from the rule box.**

I felt really tired. I stayed up till midnight to celebrate the new year.

> Workbook page 55

THiNK VALUES

Doing good

1 **Work in groups of four. You are going to run an internet fundraising challenge for a charity. Use the points below to help you organise your ideas.**

1. Decide on a charity.
   - Why are you choosing this charity?
   - What will the charity use this money for?
2. Decide on a challenge
   - What is the challenge?
   - How are people chosen for the challenge?
   - What do you have to do if you refuse to do it?
3. Think of a famous person to get involved.
   - Why this person?
   - What do you want them to do?
4. Extras
   - What other things can you do to help your campaign? (T-shirts, write a song, etc.)

2 **SPEAKING** Present your ideas to the class. Each student in your group should talk about one of the points above.

61

Literature

1 Look at the photos and read the introduction to the extract. What do you think Vic is thinking about when he's on the bus with Ingrid?

2 🔊 1.36 Read and listen to the extract and check your ideas.

A kind of loving by Stan Barstow

Vic Brown is a young draughtsman at an engineering works in northern England in the 1950s. He lives with his mother and father. He is attracted to one of the secretaries at the engineering works – Ingrid Rothwell – and one day, as they leave work, they run into each other and start walking to the bus stop together.

'I'm going your way,' she says.

I hold the door open for her and get a gorgeous whiff of her scent as she goes by. We say good night to the commissionaire and walk off down the lane. […]

It seems there's a lot I don't know and she starts to bring me up to date. I don't have to make the conversation tonight; she just rolls it out. She's as full of scandal as the Sunday papers and by the time we get to the bus stop I know more about the people who work at Whittaker's than I've learned all the time I've been there.

I get both fares into town and she says, 'That makes us quits,' and smiles.

She picks up where she left off and starts chattering again; but I'm not really listening now. My mind's working like mad on how I can make the most of this chance. I try to think of a way to get started and all the time the bus is tearing down the road into town. When I see the Grammar School sail by I kind of panic because I know we'll be in the station any minute now.

'Look, there's something I –' And she starts talking again at the same time. We both stop. 'Go on,' I say.

'I was just going to ask you if you'd seen that new musical *Rise and Shine* at the Palace,' she says. 'I was wondering what it was like.'

I haven't a clue what it's like, to be honest, but I say, 'I think it's good,' and I'm thinking, Now, now, now: what are you waiting for? 'I was thinking of going to see it myself one night this week, as a matter of fact,' I say. This is another fib, but I don't care. I have to clear my throat. 'P'raps … er, mebbe you'd like to come with me … see it together …'

She says, 'Oh!' just as if it was the last thing she'd have thought of and I begin to think how I can pass it off if she turns me down. 'Well, when?'

I can hardly sit still in the seat. I want to jump up and shout, I'm that excited. 'I'd thought of going tomorrow, but any night 'ud suit me really.'

'Tomorrow's New Year's Eve,' she says, 'and I'm going to a party. Can you make it Wednesday?'

'All right.' Wednesday, Thursday, Friday, Saturday or Sunday. I can make it any night or all of them. I just want it to be soon.

'Wednesday, then,' she says, and I nod. 'Wednesday.'

Before the bus pulls into the station we've fixed up what time we'll meet and where and everything. And to think, only this morning I wouldn't have given a bent penny for my chances. But that's how things work out sometimes. Wednesday … I just don't know how I'll live till then.

But course I do, and now here I am waiting on the corner at twenty-five to eight. She's late, but only five minutes, and I was here ten minutes early to make sure I didn't miss her so that makes it seem more.

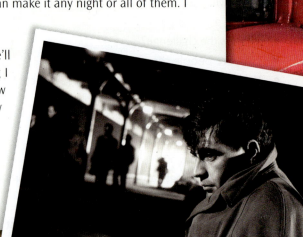

6 BRINGING PEOPLE TOGETHER

3 Read the extract again. Answer the questions.
1. What does Ingrid talk about as she and Vic walk to the bus stop?
2. What is Vic thinking about as the bus approaches the station?
3. What two things does Vic say to Ingrid that aren't really true?
4. Why does Vic want 'to jump up and shout'?
5. Why does it seem to Vic that Ingrid is later than she is?

4 VOCABULARY Match the highlighted words and phrases in the extract with the definitions.
1. a lie; something someone says that's not true
2. agreeing that no one owes anything to another person
3. things about other people that are shocking
4. be available (to meet, or to do something)
5. someone who does drawings of machines, new buildings, etc.
6. a slight smell
7. going very, very fast
8. talking a long time about not very important things

5 SPEAKING Work in pairs. Discuss the questions.
1. Vic doesn't find it easy to ask Ingrid out. Can you think of other times when people find it difficult to say what they want to say?
2. Do you think Ingrid will turn up to meet Vic? Why (not)?

WRITING
An essay

1 Read the essay quickly. Does the author agree or disagree with the essay title? Why?

2 Read the paragraph functions and write A–D in the boxes below.
1. introduction
2. argument supporting the idea
3. argument against the idea
4. the writer's final opinion

3 Complete with the missing linkers, then check in the essay.
1. _____, because it has become much easier, more and more people are trying to collect money for charity.
2. _____, people are getting tired of constantly being asked to donate each time they check their email accounts.
3. _____, these requests often come from people we don't really know. They lack the personal touch.
4. _____, people are starting to ignore these charity emails.
5. _____, I still believe that social media can be a really useful way of raising money for charity.
6. _____ it's no surprise that more and more people are using social media to raise money for charity.

4 Look at the following essay title and make notes.

Social media brings people together.

Introduction: _____
For: _____
Against: _____
My conclusion: _____

5 Write your essay in 140–190 words.

Social media is the best way of raising money for charity.

A. Nevertheless, I still believe that social media can be a really useful way of raising money for charity. We just need to be careful how we use it and make sure we don't use it too often.

B. When my mother was a child she used to take part in sponsored challenges to raise money. She would knock on people's doors asking them to promise money. Then, when she had completed the task, she had to return to collect the money. These days people use sites such as JustGiving to ask for sponsorship. With one click people can donate immediately. There's no dispute that social media is probably the most efficient way of reaching a lot of people very quickly.

C. However, because it has become much easier, more and more people are trying to collect money for charity. As a consequence, people are getting tired of constantly being asked to donate each time they check their email accounts. Furthermore, these requests often come from people we don't really know. They lack the personal touch. As a result, people are starting to ignore these charity emails.

D. These days social media is a huge part of almost everyone's life. It's often the quickest and easiest way of keeping in touch with friends or sending your message to a wide audience. Therefore it's no surprise that more and more people are using social media to raise money for charity. But is it always a good idea?

CAMBRIDGE ENGLISH: First

THiNK EXAMS

READING AND USE OF ENGLISH
Part 7: Matching

Workbook page 61

1 You are going to read an article in which four teenagers talk about how they met their best friend. For questions 1–10, choose from the teenagers (A–D). The teenagers may be chosen more than once.

Which teenager

1. feels that they met their best friend at the perfect time?
2. has changed their attitudes to best friends several times?
3. has known their best friend for most of their life?
4. felt an instant connection with their best friend?
5. thinks it can be a good thing to have a small number of very close friends?
6. gets on with their best friend because they can discuss different topics?
7. feels that their best friend also helped them to get on better with people at school?
8. thinks that distance helps keep a relationship healthy?
9. made best friends with the new kid in class straight away?
10. thinks it's a good thing that their best friend doesn't know their other friends?

A Dom

My best friend is Liam and I've only known him for about three months. I met Liam at a youth club and I knew immediately that he was going to be a great friend. We share exactly the same sense of humour. We like the same bands. I'm quite interested in politics and he shares exactly the same concerns as I do. It was great to finally be able to talk about something other than football and girls. Don't get me wrong, I still like talking about those things, but it's good to have a change. Also, because Liam doesn't go to the same school as me, it means that we don't waste time talking about other friends.

B Janice

I've had a lot of best friends. I remember when I was a kid I'd have a new best friend every week. Then when I was a bit older, I thought it was silly to have one best friend and just tried to have as many friends as I could. Recently though, I realise that although it's good to have lots of friends, it's good to have one or two extra special ones that you know will always be there for you no matter what. I guess at the moment Chloe would be that friend. I really haven't known her very long, probably about a year at the most. She was the new kid in school and at first I wasn't very friendly to her at all, probably because I already had my gang of friends. But she was in lots of my classes and I started to get to know her better and realised she was really cool.

C Anna

I still remember the first time I met Robin. I must have been about ten or eleven. I was at school when the teacher introduced him as the new student and told him to sit next to me. We started chatting immediately and have hardly stopped talking since. Mum says I didn't have a lot of friends at that age and I found it difficult to get on with the other kids. She says that Robin helped me find the confidence I needed to make new friends. Now we're at secondary school and we still spend lots of time together. Of course, I tend to hang out with the girls and Robin hangs out with the boys but we often meet up after school or at the weekend.

D Colin

I've known my best friend Tom since I was two. Of course, I don't remember him from then but we met because our dads took us to the same park to play when we were toddlers. They became best friends and we grew up almost as brothers. When I was about seven, Mum and Dad moved away but they kept in touch with Tom's parents so Tom and I would still see each other most holidays. These days we keep in touch on Facebook and we text each other loads. It's great having someone who knows you so well and I think the fact that we live more than 100 km apart has meant that we've become even better friends because we really value the time we have together. We don't get tired of each other because we're not living in each other's pockets.

TEST YOURSELF

UNITS 5 & 6

VOCABULARY

1 **Complete the sentences with the words in the list. There are four extra words.**

stream | backup | zip | upgrade | craze | split | introduced | going
recommendation | confessed | access | startled | complained | lens

1. Jake is feeling really down. He's just _____ up with his girlfriend.
2. My friends Alex and Nancy have been _____ out together for over a year.
3. I asked him four times to give me my watch back, and then he _____ that he'd lost it.
4. I know who Paul is, but I've never been _____ to him.
5. The file was so big that I had to _____ it to send it by email.
6. My computer runs my new graphics program very slowly. I need to _____ it.
7. I almost lost everything when my computer crashed, but luckily I had a _____ of most of it.
8. The old lady was so _____ when the dog jumped up at her that she dropped her shopping.
9. The neighbours _____ about the noise at our party.
10. Steve said this tablet was great, so I bought it on his _____.

/10

GRAMMAR

2 **Complete the sentences with the phrases in the list. There are two extra phrases.**

succeeded in | needn't have | been able | managed to | nowhere near as
wasn't allowed to | even though | didn't need to

1. I've never visited the museum _____ I live very close to it.
2. My uncle had loads of lessons, but he never _____ learning to drive.
3. My mum _____ go out with friends until she was 16.
4. The sequel is _____ good as the first film.
5. Dave had already asked Mum about the trip, so I _____ asked her.
6. My aunt hurt her hand last month. She hasn't _____ to play the piano since then.

3 **Find and correct the mistake in each sentence.**

1. We ran as fast as we could but we didn't manage get there in time.
2. Despite he earns a good salary, Mario says he never has enough money.
3. Nicole's parents weren't as strict with her brother than they were with her.
4. Nevertheless Barry's French isn't great, he understood a lot of the film.
5. It is very kind of you, but you don't need pick me up at my house. I can walk to the restaurant.
6. James always does well in tests, although never studying.

/12

FUNCTIONAL LANGUAGE

4 **Choose the correct options.**

1. A I think Paolo Nutini's latest album is *far and away / miles* the best album he's ever released.
   B I agree. It's *lot / even* better than his second album.
2. A I *must / need* go home now, I still have homework to finish for tomorrow.
   B No, don't be silly! You *mustn't / don't need to* do it for tomorrow – it's a holiday.
3. A Do your parents *let / allow* you stay out as late as you want?
   B Yes, but only at the weekends and I *have / must* to tell them what time I'll be home.
4. A I love this game – it's *easily / even* the best game I've ever played.
   B No way! 'Prince of Shadows' is a *whole / good* lot better than this.

/8

MY SCORE /30

22 – 30
10 – 21
0 – 9

7 ALWAYS LOOK ON THE BRIGHT SIDE

OBJECTIVES

FUNCTIONS: cheering someone up
GRAMMAR: ways of referring to the future (review); future continuous; future perfect
VOCABULARY: phrases to talk about the future: *about to*, *off to*, *on the point of*; feelings about future events

READING

1 Look at the photos. What do they mean to you? Can you relate them to a real life situation?

2 **SPEAKING** Read statements A and B. Discuss the differences in their reactions, in class. Then say who is more like you: the person who wrote statement A, or the one who wrote B.

   A My best friend has moved to another country. I'll never get over it. I won't find anybody that I like as much as her, so I won't even try to find a new friend. Imagine I found one, and she moved away too!

   B My best friend has moved to another country. That's great for her. I'm definitely going to stay in touch and I'm looking forward to hearing stories of her new life. And who knows, one day I might even be able to visit her.

3 Read through the blog quickly and answer the questions.
   1 What does the blogger call her character?
   2 What does he do for a living?
   3 Is he an optimist or a pessimist?

4 ◀)) 2.02 Read the blog again and listen. Mark the statements T (true) or F (false). Then work with a partner and correct the false statements.
   1 The blogger is concerned with her own attitudes and those of her friends.
   2 The main reason the blogger writes this post is to share an exciting story.
   3 The main character of the story is a man whose attitude to life changed after he was attacked.
   4 The robber got into the shop intending to kill the man who worked there.
   5 On the way to hospital, the man was feeling calm because of the support he got from the paramedics.
   6 When the man arrived in the operating theatre, the staff didn't seem hopeful.
   7 The man made a joke but no one found it funny.
   8 The blogger thinks that the positive attitude the man showed in a difficult situation helped to save his life.

5 **SPEAKING** Work in pairs. Discuss the questions.
   1 Did you like the story the blogger used? Do you agree that Jim's positive attitude helped save his life?
   2 Do you think a story like this could change people's attitudes? Say why (not).

7 ALWAYS LOOK ON THE BRIGHT SIDE

Me, Myself & My Take on the World

Take #17: It's all about the positivity

Today's take is all about attitude. So many of my friends are often pessimistic. You know, the kind of people who always think, 'There's a dark cloud up there. It's going to rain soon!' Guys, we all need to work on our attitudes. It matters how we see things!

I read a story recently that I want to share with you, and if you're a pessimist, maybe it'll change your attitude a bit too. It's about this guy, I've forgotten his name, let's call him Jim. He was kind of a born optimist, always in a good mood.

Jim owned a shop, and a customer once asked him how he managed to stay so friendly and positive all the time. His answer was: 'When I wake up in the morning, I know that the day will have good and bad moments for me, but whatever happens, I'm going to choose to be in a good mood.'

Then one day, something terrible happened. An armed robber came in, held him up at gunpoint and made Jim open the safe. As he was trying to open it, Jim's hand slipped. The robber saw this, probably thought, 'He's about to attack me!' and panicked and fired.

Jim was still conscious when the ambulance arrived, and he was rushed to hospital. In the ambulance, he'd felt fine because the paramedic kept telling him, 'Don't worry. I'm sure you'll be OK. As soon as we get to the hospital, the doctors will take care of you!' But once Jim was in the operating theatre and he saw the faces of the doctors and nurses, he had the feeling that people thought he was more or less dead already. He knew he needed to do something.

There was a nurse who was asking him lots of questions, very fast. One question was: 'Are you allergic to anything?' 'Yes!' Jim said loudly and everybody stopped what they were doing. There was total silence. 'Bullets!' Jim said, and all the doctors and nurses burst out laughing. And then Jim added, 'Please operate on me thinking that I'll live, and not that I'll die!'

Jim survived, thanks to the skill of the doctors and nurses. But what helped too was that he managed to remain an optimist even in the most dramatic moment of his life.

So listen up, dear readers. Let's try and think positively more often. Actually, I'm on the point of doing this right now. I'm having a piano lesson later today. Not my choice really, it's my parents who think it's good for me to learn a musical instrument. But I'll be a good girl. I'll keep an open mind. I'll choose to find something positive about playing the piano. Anyway, I'd better go. My bus leaves in five minutes. Oh, and I'm off to Spain on Tuesday for a family holiday so I guess I'll post my next update two weeks from now.

TRAIN TO THiNK

Learning to see things from a different perspective

How we see a situation influences how we feel about it and how we behave in it. Learning to look at things from a more optimistic perspective can have a positive influence on the outcome of a situation.

1 Read what these people have experienced when trying to look at things from a different perspective. Say what and who helped them change their attitude.

> *For a long time, I used to worry about everything all the time. I even used to worry about not finding anything to worry about. Then we had this discussion in class, and one of my teachers told us a saying I'll never forget. It may sound ridiculous, but it really helped me change my attitude. It basically says, 'For every problem under the sun, there is either a solution or there is none. If there is one, think till you find it. If there is none, then never mind it.'*

> *I tended not to believe in myself. I always thought everybody else was better than me. One day I went out with a group of friends, and we met this guy who seemed quite nice. But then I noticed that he started to make fun of the things I said. I became quiet and started to feel bad about myself. When I spoke to my best friend afterwards, she just said, 'So what? That guy's strange but that's him, not you.' So I decided to ignore the guy and he soon stopped making fun of me. More importantly, I felt better about myself.*

2 **SPEAKING** Think of any difficult situations where you could usefully apply either of the two perspectives above. Discuss with a partner.

67

GRAMMAR
Ways of referring to the future (review)

1 Look at the sentences from the blog. Then complete the rule with *be going to*, *will*, *the present continuous* or *the present simple*.

1 There's a dark cloud up there. It**'s going to** rain soon!
2 **I'm having** a piano lesson later today.
3 **As soon as** we **get** to the hospital, the doctors **will** take care of you!
4 **I'll** post my next update two weeks from now.
5 My bus **leaves** in five minutes.
6 Don't worry. I'm sure **you'll** be OK.
7 Whatever happens, **I'm going to** choose to be in a good mood.
8 When I wake up in the morning, I know that the day **will have** good and bad moments for me.

> **RULE:** We use:
> 1 _____ to talk about future facts.
> 2 _____ to talk about events that are part of a timetable or schedule.
> 3 _____ to make evidence-based predictions.
> 4 _____ to make predictions based on thoughts and opinions.
> 5 _____ to talk about plans and intentions.
> 6 _____ to refer to definite arrangements.
> 7 _____ immediately after time expressions like *when*, *before*, *after*, *until*, and *as soon as* when referring to future events.
> 8 _____ to refer to spontaneous decisions and offers.

2 Complete the sentences using the most appropriate form of the verbs in brackets. Sometimes more than one form is possible.

1 My dad _____ on the eight o'clock flight from Mexico City tomorrow. (arrive)
2 Careful! You've filled that glass too full. You _____ it. (spill)
3 I think it _____ probably _____ a lot this weekend. It's that time of year. (rain)
4 We _____ friends on Saturday afternoon. (see)
5 I'm sorry, I have to finish now. The film _____ in two minutes. (start)
6 We'll stop at the market before we _____ home. (go)
7 When I get paid, I _____ myself a new camera. (buy)
8 Today's lunch break _____ five minutes shorter than usual. (be)

➡ Workbook page 64

VOCABULARY
Phrases to talk about the future: *about to, off to, on the point of*

1 All of these sentences refer to the future. Which sentence talks about:

a future travel plans?
b the very immediate future (x2)

1 He**'s about to** attack me.
2 I**'m off** to Spain on Tuesday.
3 I**'m on the point of** doing this right now.

> **LOOK!**
> - *be about to* + infinitive
> - *be off to* + infinitive / noun
> - *be on the point of* + verb + *-ing*

2 Choose the correct options.

1 Although this is a serious situation, Jennifer looks as if she's *about to / off to* start laughing.
2 I'm *off to / about to* the supermarket in five minutes. Do you want anything?
3 Careful! You're *off to / about to* knock the glass over.
4 My friends are *off to / about to* get a big surprise!
5 They're *off to / on the point of* France on holiday next month.
6 It's 2–0, there's only one minute left – wow, we're *on the point of / about to* winning the match!

➡ Workbook page 66

LISTENING

1 🔊 2.03 Listen to the radio show *Silver Linings* and answer the questions.

1 Complete the phrase: 'Every _____ has a silver lining'.
2 Explain this phrase in your own words.

2 🔊 2.03 Listen again and note down Dan's and Anna's answers for each round.

Round 1
Dan: _____
Anna: _____

Round 2
Dan: _____
Anna: _____

3 **SPEAKING** Work in pairs. Who would you give the points to in each situation (Anna or Dan) and why?

7 ALWAYS LOOK ON THE BRIGHT SIDE

GRAMMAR
Future continuous

1 **Look at the examples from the recording. Then choose the correct option in the rule and complete with *be* and *-ing*.**

   1 On Tuesday afternoon my friends **will be playing** football.
   2 **I'll be sitting** in the new ice cream shop near school, enjoying a delicious ice cream.

   > **RULE:** To talk about an action that will be in progress ¹*after / around* a specific future time, we use the future continuous: will + ² _____ + the ³ _____ form of the verb.
   >
   > **I'll be sitting** in the new ice cream shop.

2 **Complete the conversation with the correct form of the verb in brackets – future simple or future continuous.**

   JESSIE This time tomorrow, my dad and I ¹_____ (sit) on a train.
   PAULA   Really? Where are you going? Anywhere nice?
   JESSIE Yes. Dad's invited me to go to London with him on Saturday.
   PAULA   Wow!
   JESSIE Tomorrow morning we ²_____ (walk) around the city doing a bit of shopping.
   PAULA   Great! I ³_____ (phone) you on Saturday afternoon.
   JESSIE Well, that's not really a good time. On Saturday afternoon we ⁴_____ (watch) the football match. Chelsea against Arsenal. I can't wait! You know how much I like football.
   PAULA   And you ⁵_____ (come) home happy and relaxed. Lucky you.
   JESSIE Well I hope so. It's an important game for Chelsea.
   PAULA   It all sounds wonderful. So what time's your train tomorrow?
   JESSIE 6 o'clock.
   PAULA   Alright. At 6.30, I ⁶_____ (think) of you.
   JESSIE And I ⁷_____ (put) some photos from our weekend on Facebook – if I remember.

Future perfect

3 **Look at the example sentences and complete the rule with *have*, *past participle* and *will*.**

   1 By the time the plane leaves London, a lot of snow **will have fallen** on our ski resort in Italy.
   2 Anna will still be shopping in Heathrow and she**'ll have missed** her flight.

   > **RULE:** To talk about an action that will finish some time between now and a specified time in the future, we use the future perfect. We often use it with the preposition *by*:
   > ¹_____ + ²_____ + ³_____
   >
   > By then, **I'll have become** a big basketball star.

4 **Choose the correct tense to complete the sentences.**

   1 By the time Mum comes back from work, I will *be finishing / have finished* my homework.
   2 By 2030, psychologists will *be finding / have found* ways to help pessimists feel more optimistic.
   3 Don't call after 10 pm. I will *be sleeping / have slept*.
   4 This time tomorrow morning I will *be flying / have flown* to Singapore. We land in the afternoon.
   5 When I leave this school, I will *be spending / have spent* six years there.
   6 You can find Miss Green in classroom 3. She will *be teaching / have taught* there until midday.
   7 We're going to watch films all day Saturday. By the end of the day, we will *be watching / have watched* more than five films!
   8 The band will *be touring / have toured* for six months later this year to promote their new album.

   Workbook page 65

SPEAKING

1 **Work in groups of four and play *Silver Linings*. Read the situations and think of optimistic solutions. Make notes.**

   • Student A: Your best friend completely forgets your birthday.
   • Student B: Someone pours orange juice over your new T-shirt.
   • Student C: You fail your History exam.
   • Student D: Your country doesn't qualify for the football World Cup.

2 **Take turns to talk about the 'silver linings' in your situations. Give a point for each correct use of the future continuous or the future perfect. Award five points for the most imaginative answer.**

READING

1 Read this website page. Who is it for? What are the two worries mentioned by people who've posted on the website?

2 Read again. Match the answers with the worries. There is one extra quote.

3 Read again. Answer the questions.
   1 What does the writer have in common with the two worriers?
   2 What is the difference between the writer and the two worriers?
   3 Are the two worriers equally pessimistic? Why (not)?
   4 What is the writer referring to in the third answer by saying 'And remember the rainbow!'?

4 **SPEAKING** Discuss in class.
   1 What kind of person is the owner of this website? Would you like to get to know them? Why (not)?
   2 Do you think quotations can cheer you up when you're down?
   3 How would you react if you were in the situation of one of the two worriers?
   4 Which of the three quotes do you like most? Why?
   5 Look at the extra quote. What kind of problem could this quote be an answer to?

QUOTATIONSforWORRIERS

'You'll never find a rainbow if you look down!' Who said that? No, it wasn't me. It was Charlie Chaplin, and I love it. You must know that I wasn't exactly born an optimist myself. I was actually quite a worrier until I discovered the power of inspirational quotes. Try me. Send me a worry, and I'll send you a quote. For free. If you like the quote, please let me know. Positive messages help me too.

A shallIstayorshallIgo?

Hi, I don't know what to do. I've got an uncle in the USA, and he and his wife have invited me to go there next summer. Sounds cool, doesn't it? But I'm worried there won't be anyone my age to hang out with. They live in a smallish sort of town, and they haven't got any kids themselves. It may sound weird, but I feel that whatever I decide, I'll probably regret it later!

B Drummer boy

Help needed! I got this drum kit for my 16th birthday. There's a band at my school. They're great, but their drummer, Keith, is leaving at the end of the school year – his family is moving to another town. The band have asked me if I want to audition and Keith has offered to teach me. But I'm not sure I'll be good enough. I don't think I should get my hopes up. I'd be so disappointed if I didn't get in.

1 ☐ Mmh. Yes, I understand that's not an easy situation. But I don't think that means you should just sit around complaining that everything's gloomy. Maybe what Anne Frank said will help you to be more optimistic: 'How wonderful it is that nobody needs to wait a single moment before starting to improve the world.'

2 ☐ Look, this is for you, and it's by Mahatma Ghandi. I'll say no more. It's all in the quote. 'Man often becomes what he believes himself to be. If I keep on saying to myself that I cannot do a certain thing, it is possible that I may end by really becoming incapable of doing it. On the contrary, if I have the belief that I can do it, I shall surely acquire the capacity to do it even if I may not have it at the beginning.'

3 ☐ My quote for you is by Winston Churchill: 'A pessimist sees the difficulty in every opportunity; an optimist sees the opportunity in every difficulty.' Even if you are right, there are probably about a million things you can do there that you can't do at home! So I'd say, go. And remember the rainbow!

7 ALWAYS LOOK ON THE BRIGHT SIDE

VOCABULARY
Feelings about future events

1 Work in pairs. Make a list of five situations or events which can make you feel worried.

2 Read the following extracts from quotationsforworriers. What event do you think each extract refers to?

A It's a big game and **I'm feeling quite apprehensive**. If we win, we'll be top of the league. I'm excited but **I'm also a bit unsure** about our chances. I mean, they're a good team.

B **I'm really looking forward to** it and **I feel quite positive** about it. If I'm honest, I'll probably be old enough to be the other students' mother and that will feel a bit odd but overall I don't care. **I've got a really good feeling about** this. Any suggestions for how I can bridge the age gap with my new classmates?

C I'm **absolutely dreading** it and I'm sure I'm going to fail. I haven't done any revision and **I just don't know where to start**. It's a nightmare – I'm really **worried** about it.

D I don't know why **I'm getting so worked up**. I've seen him loads of times before and he's really good but **I've just got a bad feeling about** it this time. I think I need to have one of my teeth taken out.

3 Look at the words in bold and use them to complete each list. If needed, use a dictionary to help you with meaning.

expressing optimism	expressing pessimism / worry
I'm really looking forward to	*I'm dreading*

4 Match the expressions in Exercise 3 with the events you listed in Exercise 1 in which you might feel them.

> Workbook page 66

FUNCTIONS
Cheering someone up

1 ◉ 2.04 Complete the sentences with the words in the list. Then listen and check.

down | cheer | light | hang | bright

1 _____ up! Things will seem better after a good night's sleep.
2 _____ in there. Your exams will be over soon.
3 Don't let it get you _____. It's not the end of the world.
4 I can see that losing the match is really bothering you, but try to look on the _____ side – it's early in the season.
5 I know this year of high school can be really difficult, but there is _____ at the end of the tunnel. We've got holidays next month.

2 Work in pairs. What would you say to each person A–D in Vocabulary Exercise 2? Use the phrases in Exercise 1.

Pronunciation
Intonation: Encouraging someone
Go to page 121.

THiNK SELF-ESTEEM
What cheers me up

1 Which of these things help you feel better when you are down? Think of two more of your own.

☐ doing something outdoors
☐ talking with family
☐ chatting with a friend
☐ going to a party
☐ chocolate
☐ watching a good film
☐ shopping
☐ sleep

2 How do each of these things help cheer you up? Make notes.
doing something outdoors — forget about problems.

3 **SPEAKING** Work in pairs. Discuss your answers.

> When I've had an argument with my mum, I always like going for a long walk by myself. It helps me see things more clearly.

WRITING
A short story

You are going to write a story (140–190 words) which finishes with the words, 'Every cloud has a silver lining'.

Think of:
- an unfortunate incident.
- an unexpected positive outcome.
- how it changed the main character's life.

PHOTOSTORY: episode 3

The competition

1 **Look at the photos and answer the questions.**
  1 What do you think Liam wants to do?
  2 What does Emma think of his idea?

2 ◁)) 2.07 **Now read and listen to the photostory. Check your ideas.**

LIAM So, what about this one, Emma? This was the sunset outside our house yesterday. What do you think? Pretty amazing, isn't it?
EMMA Um. Yes, it's pretty … um. It's pretty! It's the best one you've shown me so far.
LIAM I'm really getting into photography. And I've only been doing it for two months or so. It's amazing what great photos you can get just using your phone.
EMMA Yes. Yes, I guess so.
LIAM Anyway, there's a photo competition next month at school that I'm thinking of entering. First prize is a tablet. I think I've got a really good shot.
EMMA That's great. Go for it.

EMMA Then he tells me he's thinking of entering the school photo competition. I don't want to be negative but there's no way he's good enough.
JUSTIN Yeah, he showed me some of his photos the other day too – pictures of some trees that he thought looked cool, but I wasn't that impressed. They were out of focus for a start!
NICOLE He hasn't shown me any of his photos yet. Are they really that bad?
JUSTIN I'm afraid so. They're the sort of thing you might post online and get a few 'likes' but they're certainly not going to win any competitions.
EMMA But that's just it. He thinks he's got a good chance. I don't want him to get his hopes up.
JUSTIN He's got no chance at all.
NICOLE So, what are we going to do? We can't let him make a fool of himself.
EMMA I don't know. I tried to tell him they weren't that good, gently of course, but you know Liam.
JUSTIN Yes, it can be difficult to tell him things sometimes. He's always so enthusiastic.
NICOLE Well, we have to do something.

EMMA I've got an idea.
NICOLE What?
EMMA Well, you said he hadn't shown you his photos yet. Why don't you ask to see them and then tell him the truth?
NICOLE Oh thanks. So I get to be the bad guy? And I haven't even seen them! Maybe I won't think they're bad.
EMMA Fair enough. But if you do agree with us, then you've got to stop him! It's too late for us to say anything.
JUSTIN Yeah, we can't tell him now. You have to try at least.

7 ALWAYS LOOK ON THE BRIGHT SIDE

DEVELOPING SPEAKING

3 Work in pairs. Discuss what happens next in the story. Write down your ideas.

We think Emma helps Liam by giving him some of her photos for the competition.

4 ◼ EP3 Watch to find out how the story continues.

5 Mark the statements T (true) or F (false).

1 Nicole talks to Liam but doesn't tell him what she really thinks.
2 Liam thinks Emma really likes his photos.
3 Nicole thinks Justin didn't try very hard.
4 Emma, Justin and Nicole decide to go to the photography exhibition separately.
5 Justin claims that he had previously said that Liam was a great photographer.
6 Liam took the winning photos with his phone.

PHRASES FOR FLUENCY

1 **Find these expressions in the photostory. Who says them? How do you say them in your language?**

1 Anyway, …
2 Fair enough.
3 … for a start, …
4 get (his) hopes up
5 Go for it.
6 make a fool of (himself)

2 **Match the expressions in Exercise 1 to these meanings.**

a try it
b have high expectations
c the first reason is …
d appear ridiculous to others
e I understand why you said / did that
f So, let me change the subject

3 **Use the expressions in Exercise 1, in the correct form, to complete the mini-dialogues.**

1 A Well, there are lots of reasons I don't want to go there. It's very expensive, _____.
   B _____. We'll have to think of another place to go, then.
2 A There's a singing competition at school next month. I thought I might _____.
   B Well don't _____; Susan Kenny's bound to win it.
3 A So have you decided to go for the school football team trials?
   B No, I decided not to. I'm not good enough and I'd only _____.
   A That's a shame and I'm sure that wouldn't happen.
   B _____, even if I did get in, they play on Saturday mornings and I like to lie in on Saturdays.

WordWise

Expressions with *so*

1 **Look at these sentences from the photostory. Complete them with phrases from the list.**

so far | I told you so | I'm afraid so
… or so | I guess so | So,

1 JUSTIN Liam's photos are really good! _____!
   EMMA No you didn't!
2 EMMA _____, what are we going to do?
3 NICOLE Are the photos really that bad?
   JUSTIN _____.
4 LIAM It's amazing what great photos you can get just using your phone.
   EMMA Yes. Yes, _____.
5 LIAM I've only been taking photos for two months _____.
6 EMMA This is the best photo you've shown me _____.

2 **Use expressions from Exercise 1 to complete the sentences.**

1 A _____, have you decided what you want?
   B Not yet.
2 A Is it broken?
   B Yes, _____.
3 A How long does it take to get there?
   B Not long. Twenty minutes _____.
4 A How's it going?
   B OK. I've answered six questions _____. Only four more to do.
5 A Is Jack running late?
   B _____ – he said he'd be here by now.
6 A This place is horrible.
   B Well, _____ – but you didn't listen!

➤ Workbook page 66

8 MAKING LISTS

OBJECTIVES

FUNCTIONS: saying 'Yes' and adding conditions
GRAMMAR: conditionals (review); mixed conditionals
VOCABULARY: phrasal verbs (2); alternatives to *if*: *suppose, provided, as long as, otherwise, unless*

READING

1 **SPEAKING** Look at the photos. In pairs, think of:
   1 three ways in which the jobs are different
   2 three things the jobs have in common
   3 something that connects *all* of the pictures
   Then compare your ideas with others in the class.

2 Read the book review quickly. What does Atul Gawande recommend using to ensure procedures are followed?

3 ◆) 2.08 Read the review again and listen. Match the paragraphs with the titles. There is one extra title.
   A Lives can be saved
   B It's not just for the medical profession
   C Mistakes don't really matter
   D Holes in the system
   E Not everyone agrees
   F A book for everyone

4 Answer the questions.
   1 What surprised the doctor who went into the operating theatre?
   2 What was the result of an experiment in an important American hospital?
   3 What examples does Gawande give of what could happen if engineers and pilots didn't follow checklists?
   4 How did many of the doctors react to the idea of using checklists? Why do you think they reacted this way?
   5 Why does the writer of the review recommend the book?

5 **SPEAKING** Work in pairs. Discuss the questions.
   1 Can you think of any other jobs where checklists should be compulsory?
   2 When have you made checklists for yourself? What for? Were they useful?
   3 Do you agree with the last sentence in the review? Why (not)?

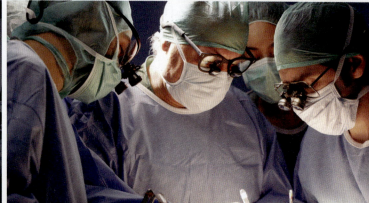

8 MAKING LISTS

The Checklist Manifesto
by
Atul Gawande

1 A doctor in a large hospital walked into an operating theatre where an operation was being performed. Everything seemed to be going well, but the doctor noticed that no one was wearing a face mask. He was surprised – wearing a face mask is basic hospital procedure. But he didn't say anything. The operation was a success but a few days later the patient came down with a fever. It turned out that she had a serious infection, probably because the doctors and nurses hadn't followed a simple rule. If they'd worn their masks, the patient wouldn't have been infected.

2 Someone who'd be interested in that story is Atul Gawande, who wrote a book called *The Checklist Manifesto: How to get things right*. Gawande is a doctor himself, and in his book he suggests that if surgeons run through a simple checklist before every operation, then lives will be saved. And he's got the numbers to prove it. In 2001, at an important American hospital, there was an experiment that required doctors to use a five-point checklist before they carried out specific procedures. The checklist was just a list of routine things doctors should normally do without thinking – for example, wearing rubber gloves, washing hands before and after every patient, and so on. By making sure that the checklist was followed, there were almost no infections over the 27 months of the experiment, and they reckon that around eight lives were saved. When the checklist was tested again in hospitals in Michigan, USA, infections went down by 66 percent.

3 In his book, Gawande looks at other professions, too, to support his argument that checklists reduce accidents and improve success rates. He points out that people like engineers and pilots use checklists all the time, and he comes up with some good examples. Just imagine that an aeroplane crashed because the pilot had failed to follow basic procedures. Suppose a skyscraper fell down because the engineers hadn't remembered to do some important calculations. There would be an immediate inquiry to look into these events. So Gawande's question is: If pilots and engineers use checklists, why don't doctors use them?

4 But when Gawande talked to doctors at eight hospitals about a checklist that he had developed, he found that a lot of them weren't very enthusiastic. Twenty percent of the doctors that Gawande talked to said that the list was too difficult to use and that it wouldn't help to save lives. But, when they were shown the statement, 'If I had surgery, I'd want the surgeon to use this list', 93 percent of the same doctors agreed with it! So it's hard to work out why they don't want to use it themselves.

5 *The Checklist Manifesto* is a really interesting and well-written book. It reminds us to do basic things to avoid problems. It's relevant for all of us, not just for doctors. We should all use checklists now and again, otherwise we'll make mistakes.

Book of the month

■ TRAIN TO THiNK ■

The 'goal setting' checklist

When you go on a journey, you wouldn't say to yourself, 'I don't know where to go to, but I'll start my journey anyway.' You will never know if your destination is where you wanted to be if you don't set yourself goals. This is important for all of our 'journeys' in life. The 'goal setting' checklist helps you think clearly about what it is you want to achieve and how you're going to achieve it.

1 Martin has a new project. He wants to learn to play the guitar. Look at these ideas that Martin has written and match them to 1–5 in the checklist below. (Some include more than one idea and some could go in more than one place in the checklist.)

   a I'll be able to play about 20 songs ☐
   b approach it as something to be enjoyed ☐
   c I'll feel really good about my achievement ☐
   d learn to play the guitar ☐
   e positive comments from family and friends ☐
   f a friend who will teach me ☐
   g discipline to practise daily ☐
   h lessons streamed from the Internet ☐

2 **SPEAKING** Think of something you want to achieve. Create a checklist to help you define your goals more clearly. Compare with a partner.

> 1 What I want to achieve
> 2 Things I need in order to achieve this goal
> 3 How I need to act or behave in order to achieve this goal
> 4 Things that tell me I have achieved this goal
> 5 Results of achieving goal for myself and others

GRAMMAR
Conditionals (review)

1 Write the correct form of the verbs in brackets and check in the book review on page 75. Then complete the table.

1 If surgeons _____ (run) through a simple checklist before every operation, then lives _____ (be) saved.
2 If they _____ (wear) their masks, the patient _____ (not be) infected.
3 If pilots and engineers _____ (use) checklists, why _____ doctors _____ (use) them?
4 If I _____ (have) surgery, I _____ (want) the surgeon to use this list.

RULE:

Type of conditional	Example sentence	If clause	Main clause
Zero	3	present simple	1 _____
First	2 _____	3 _____	4 _____
Second	5 _____	6 _____	would(n't) + infinitive
Third	7 _____	past perfect	8 _____

2 Match the four sentences a doctor might say to a patient with the situations a–d.

1 If people take this medicine, they don't get headaches.
2 If you take this medicine, you won't get headaches.
3 If you took this medicine, you wouldn't get headaches.
4 If you had taken this medicine, you wouldn't have got headaches.

a The patient didn't take the medicine.
b The doctor is telling the patient a general fact about the medicine.
c The patient isn't taking the medicine, and gets headaches.
d The doctor is telling the patient about a future result of taking the medicine.

3 Write conditional sentences.

1 Reading books is a great idea. (0 conditional)
If you / read books, you / learn things about life.
2 I think you should buy the book. (1st conditional)
You / discover interesting things about pilots and doctors if you / read it.
3 Gawande's a doctor. (2nd conditional)
If Gawande / not be a doctor, he / not understand so much about this.
4 I read this book a week or two ago. (3rd conditional)
I / not find out about the importance of checklists if I / not read it.

→ Workbook page 72

VOCABULARY
Phrasal verbs (2)

1 Use the phrases in the list to complete the sentences. Then check in the book review on page 75.

run through | points out | look into | work out
came down with | comes up with | turned out
carried out

1 The patient _____ a fever.
2 It _____ that she had a serious infection.
3 If surgeons _____ a simple checklist before every operation, then lives will be saved.
4 There was an experiment that required doctors to use a […] checklist before they _____ specific procedures.
5 Gawande _____ that people like engineers and pilots use checklists all the time.
6 He _____ some good examples.
7 There would be an immediate inquiry to _____ it.
8 It's hard to _____ why they don't want to use it [a checklist] themselves.

2 **SPEAKING** Work in pairs. Discuss the meaning of the phrasal verbs in Exercise 1.

3 Use the correct form of one of the verbs in Exercise 1 to complete each sentence.

1 The police are _____ why the accident happened.
2 My sister didn't go to school last week – she _____ a very bad cold.
3 I just can't _____ why he doesn't like me.
4 The doctors _____ some tests to see what was wrong with me.
5 I'd like to _____ that the capital of Brazil isn't São Paulo, it's Brasilia.
6 Let's _____ the names to make sure we haven't forgotten anyone.
7 I thought André was French, but he _____ to be Canadian.
8 I tried to think of some ideas for the weekend, but I didn't _____ any good ones.

→ Workbook page 74

76

8 MAKING LISTS

LISTENING
Why do we make lists?

1 **SPEAKING** Work in pairs. Look at these lists and discuss the questions.
   1 What's the purpose of each list?
   2 Why do people make lists like these?

2 🔊 2.09 Listen to an interview with a social psychologist. Which of the reasons for lists that you gave in Exercise 1 does she mention?

3 🔊 2.09 Listen again and complete the information below. Use one or two words to complete the spaces.

Katy's five reasons for making lists:
1 to _____ information
2 to aid your _____
3 to _____ your mind
4 to decrease _____
5 to make you _____ about yourself

4 **SPEAKING** Match the lists in Exercise 1 to some of the reasons in Exercise 3. Compare your ideas with a partner.

5 **SPEAKING** Which of these kinds of lists do you make? Do you agree with the psychologist about why you make them?

GRAMMAR
Mixed conditionals

1 🔊 2.10 Complete the sentences from the interview with the words or phrases in the list. Listen and check.

had | were | would have | would

1 If I _____ more organised, I _____ made a list of them I suppose.
2 If I _____ made a list, then I _____ know what to buy.

2 Look at the sentences again. Find the second and third conditional parts in each one. Then match them to the sentences in the rule.

> **RULE:** Sometimes, we mix second and third conditional forms so that we can connect present and past actions.
> - To talk about the present result of an unreal or imagined past action we use: *if* + *had* + past participle, *would* ('d) + infinitive. **Sentence** ¹_____
> - To talk about the past result of an unreal or hypothetical present situation or fact, we use: *if* + past simple, *would* ('d) *have* + past participle. **Sentence** ²_____

3 Write mixed conditional sentences to describe these situations.

0 I don't have any money. I didn't buy that phone.
If I had some money, I'd have bought that phone.
1 Anna and Dan had a big argument. They aren't talking to each other.
2 We didn't leave early. That's why we're late now.
3 I don't have a good memory. I forgot her birthday.
4 I didn't eat breakfast. Now I'm hungry.
5 He didn't pay attention. He can't do the homework.

4 Work in pairs. Use the gapped sentences. How many different mixed conditional examples can you make in two minutes?

1 If I hadn't _____ yesterday, I wouldn't be _____ now.
2 If I was _____, I would have _____.
3 I wouldn't have _____ if I didn't like _____.
4 I would _____ if I had _____ at school.

➔ Workbook page 73

Pronunciation
Weak forms with conditionals
Go to page 121.

READING

1 **SPEAKING** What 'top ten' lists have you seen (or written) recently? Tell a partner.

2 Read the blog. Answer the questions.
   1 Why is Adrian posting his own list this week?
   2 Where can you see the complete lists?
   3 What does Adrian want his readers to do?

ADRIAN'S LIST BLOG

As you know, every week I post a top ten list here that someone has sent me. Well, this week, no one has sent me anything, so I'm offering you a top ten list of … my favourite top ten lists! And here they are.

1 Top ten uses for a potato
This isn't about cooking potatoes, it's about using them for things like making electricity or improving your skin!

2 Top ten strange museums
Here are some really weird museums you can visit (as long as you have the money to travel all over the world, of course).

3 Top ten worst countries at football
If you're into football, you might like this list, unless you're from somewhere like San Marino or American Samoa (they're on the list).

4 Top ten ugly creatures
There are some great photos here that I'm sure you'll love, provided you like seriously ugly fish and animals!

5 Top ten bad science fiction films
Imagine spending a whole weekend watching really bad sci-fi films. My favourite is *Plan 9 from Outer Space* but perhaps you have other ideas.

6 Top ten actors who don't like watching their own films
Apparently Johnny Depp avoids viewing his own films. He prefers to walk away with the experience of having made the film rather than focussing on the end product – and he's not alone.

7 Top ten unexplained mysteries
Surprisingly, the Nazca lines in Peru and the Easter Island statues do not appear on this list, but there are ten other really strange mysteries from around the world.

8 Top ten stupid criminals
The bank robber who wrote 'Give me the money!' on an envelope with his name and address on it? He's just one of the hopeless criminals on this great list.

9 Top ten weird world records
What's the world record for the number of T-shirts being worn by one person at the same time? And more things like that. (The answer, by the way, is 245.)

10 Top ten signs in badly written English
Suppose you were in another country and saw a sign in a shop that said: 'Wee spik Inglish hear'. You'd laugh out loud! If you like that kind of thing, you'll love this list!

So, that's me done for this week. You can find these lists in my archive. Lastly – please send me a list, people, otherwise I won't have anything for next week.

3 Which list do each of these sentences come from? Write a number (1–10) in the boxes.
   a The dog with the longest ears is Tigger – his ears are each about 30 centimetres long.
   b This place, in Avanos in Turkey, has a huge collection of hair from over 16,000 people – and, it's all in a small cave.
   c If you cut one in half and rub it on your shoes, your shoes will look great.
   d There are some beautiful animals in Africa – but the warthog isn't one of them!
   e Near the bottom of the list are the Turks and Caicos Islands, where cricket is much more popular.

4 **SPEAKING** Which five lists would you like to read in full? Compare your ideas with a partner.

5 **SPEAKING** Choose one of these sentence stems, add a word or words at the end and make a list. Or, make a different list altogether. Write your list and then discuss with the class.

My top five most interesting …
My top five worst …
My top five strangest …
My top five funniest …

8 MAKING LISTS

THiNK VALUES
Lists

1 **Tick the sentences you agree with.**

☐ 1 I never waste my time reading top ten lists.
☐ 2 Top ten lists aren't meant to be taken seriously – just enjoy them!
☐ 3 Some top ten lists can be very useful.
☐ 4 People who write top ten lists must have very high opinions of themselves.

2 **SPEAKING** Compare your choices with others in the class.

3 **Which of these top ten lists would interest you? Put a tick (✓) or a cross (✗). Add one more thing of your own that you think would make for an interesting top ten list.**

1 someone's favourite songs ☐
2 things to do at the weekend in your town ☐
3 books to read ☐
4 things to do before you're twenty ☐
5 ways to make money ☐
6 things to do to relax and be happy ☐
7 _____ ☐

VOCABULARY
Alternatives to *if*: *suppose, provided, as long as, otherwise, unless*

> **LOOK!**
> - to hypothesise about the present: *suppose* + past simple, *would* + infinitive
> - to talk about a future possibility and its results: *as long as* / *unless* + present simple, *will* + infinitive

1 **Match the sentence halves from the blog.**

1 **Suppose** you were in another country and saw this sign in a shop ☐
2 You can visit these museums, ☐
3 You might like this list, ☐
4 I'll post your list, ☐
5 Please send me a list, ☐

a **provided** it hasn't been done before.
b **as long as** you have the money to travel.
c – you'd laugh out loud.
d **otherwise** I won't have anything for next week.
e **unless** you're from San Marino or American Samoa.

2 **Which of the words in bold in Exercise 1 means:**

1 but only if *as long as* / _____
2 imagine _____
3 if … not … _____
4 because if not _____

3 **Choose the correct options.**

1 I don't mind going to the cinema alone *unless* / *provided* / *otherwise* it's a film I really want to see.
2 I think I should go home now, *unless* / *provided* / *otherwise* my parents will be worried.
3 You'll do fine in the exam *unless* / *provided* / *suppose* you study enough.
4 I'll never speak to you again *otherwise* / *unless* / *provided* you say sorry right now!
5 OK, I'll tell you what happened, *as long as* / *suppose* / *unless* you promise not to tell anyone else!
6 *Suppose* / *Provided* / *Unless* you weren't at school today. What would you do?

→ Workbook page 74

FUNCTIONS
Saying 'Yes' and adding conditions

1 **Work in pairs. Read the sentences and discuss who is talking to whom and what they are talking about.**

1 You can borrow it if you drive really carefully. (as long as)
2 Yes, you can go to the party, if you promise to be home by 11 o'clock. (provided)
3 If you don't help me, I'll get really bad marks. (unless)
4 I'll fix it if you let me play games on it. (as long as)
5 Close the door, or it'll get cold in here. (otherwise)
6 Yes, you can practise if you don't make a lot of noise. (provided)
7 Imagine you could play the guitar – what kind of music would you play? (suppose)

2 **Now rewrite the sentences in Exercise 1, using the words in brackets.**

3 **A friend asks you these things. For each one, on what conditions would you say yes? Make notes.**

1 Can I use your phone to make a call?
   no international phone calls / no long phone calls
2 Will you come shopping with me?
3 Please come to the football match with me.
4 Can I borrow your jacket, please?

4 **Use your notes in Exercise 3. Write your answers. Then work with a partner and act out the conversations for the situations.**

> *Yes, all right – as long as / provided you don't make any long calls on it.*

79

Culture

1 Centuries ago, there was a list of the 'Seven Wonders of the Ancient World'. Do you know any of the things or places that were on that list?

2 **2.13** Read and listen to the article about the New Seven Wonders of the World. Which one is:
   - the oldest?
   - the newest?

The New Seven Wonders of the World

Recently, an online poll was held to choose the New Seven Wonders of the World. Over 100 million people voted. Here are the seven winners – in no particular order.

Chichén Itzá, Yucatan Peninsula, Mexico

This was an important city for the Mayans between about 800 and 1200 CE. A symbol of Mayan civilisation, it was a centre for trade in things like cloth, honey and salt. Most photographs of Chichén Itzá show a 24-metre high pyramid called El Castillo. There is also a ruin known as El Caracol which the Mayans used as an observatory – the view of the night sky from the top is beautiful.

Christ the Redeemer, Rio de Janeiro, Brazil

Built between 1922 and 1931, the 'Cristo Redentor' statue on Mount Corcovado has become a worldwide icon of Brazil. Constructed of concrete and soapstone, the statue is about thirty metres high (and stands on an eight-metre pedestal) and the outstretched arms measure 28 metres end to end. Designed by a Frenchman and built by Heitor da Silva Costa, it attracts thousands of visitors every year.

The Colosseum, Rome, Italy

This famous amphitheatre, built between 70 CE and 80 CE, was used by the Romans for about 500 years for all kinds of public spectacles. Now it is almost a complete ruin, as a result of earthquakes and the passage of time, but some parts can be visited. The Colosseum has become one of the most famous images of Italy.

Great Wall of China, China

This amazing structure was built over a period of more than two thousand years, ending in the 16th century. It was built in order to keep out the hostile tribes of Mongolia on the other side. The Great Wall is not actually just one continuous wall, but a succession of many different ones. At around 6,500 kilometres, it's the longest man-made structure on the planet.

Machu Picchu, Peru

Sitting up high in the Andes, the Inca city of Machu Picchu is believed to have been a sacred place for the inhabitants of nearby Cusco. The Incas built it in the mid-1400s, though we don't really know how. The Incas abandoned the city and for many years, only local people knew about it, until it was rediscovered in 1911. Many tourists go there, mostly by train from Cusco.

Petra, Jordan

The city of Petra flourished from nine BCE to 40 CE. It was the capital of the Nabataea Empire. The city was built in a desert area by the people of this civilisation, who were very skilled at finding and storing water. There are many buildings carved out of stone, an amphitheatre that held 4,000 people and a monastery. Petra became a World Heritage Site in 1985.

Taj Mahal, Agra, India

Built of white marble between 1632 and 1648, the world-famous Taj Mahal is thought of as one of the most beautiful buildings in the world. It's a mixture of Persian, Islamic, Turkish and Indian styles. It was built by Emperor Shah Jahan as the place to bury his wife Mumtaz Mahal when she died. Inside, there are flower gardens and pools.

3 Which place or thing:
   1 is in a desert?
   2 has architecture from different places mixed together?
   3 has been damaged by natural events?
   4 was designed to protect the people who built it?
   5 was built in ways we don't really understand?
   6 took nine years to construct?
   7 was used to look at the stars?

8 MAKING LISTS

4 VOCABULARY Match the highlighted words in the article to the definitions.

1. left the place for ever and never went back
2. put something into a hole in the ground
3. grew, developed very successfully
4. unfriendly and aggressive, wanting to attack
5. a famous thing or person that represents a group or country
6. exciting public shows or events
7. one thing coming after another
8. made by cutting

SPEAKING

Discuss in pairs or small groups.

1. Imagine you could choose one of the seven wonders to go and see. Which one would it be and why?
2. Think of two things from your country that you could campaign to be included in a list of seven wonders of the world. Give reasons to support your choice.

WRITING

Essay

1 Read Javed's essay. Why does he think the Simplon Tunnel is a modern wonder of the world?

2 Read the essay again. Ten things are underlined. Five of the things are mistakes, the other five are correct. Find an example of:

- a spelling mistake
- a mistake with the verb tense
- a mistake with the wrong choice of connecting word
- a preposition mistake
- a mistake which is a missing word

3 Correct the mistakes in Javed's writing.

4 Look again at the list of kinds of mistakes in Exercise 2.

1. Are there other kinds of mistakes that people make in writing? What are they? (e.g. punctuation, …)
2. Does the list in Exercise 2 show the kinds of mistakes that you have sometimes made in your writing so far using this book? If you've made other kinds of mistake, what were they?
3. Make a checklist for yourself of 'Mistakes I should try not to make when I write in English'.

5 You're going to write an essay entitled: 'A Modern Wonder of the World'.

1. Look at question 2 in the Speaking exercise above. Choose one of the things that you discussed there.
2. Make notes about why you think this thing is a good choice for a modern wonder of the world.

6 Write your essay in 150–200 words.

- Make sure you state clearly what your choice is, and say where and what it is.
- Give reasons for your choice being a 'wonder of the world'.
- When you have written your text, read it through again and use your checklist of personal mistakes (Exercise 4.3) to make as sure as possible that there are no mistakes in your writing.

A Modern Wonder of the World: The Simplon Tunnel

My choice for a modern wonder of the world is the Simplon Tunnel ¹ <u>at</u> Switzerland. It's actually two tunnels – railway tracks run through both of them. They're each almost twenty kilometres long, so they're not ² <u>…</u> longest tunnels in the world now, but they were when they were built, back in the beginning ³ <u>of</u> the twentieth century. The first one was started in 1898 and opened in 1906. The other one was started in 1912 and was opened in 1921, so each one ⁴ <u>has taken</u> about eight years to construct.

The first tunnel was built by drilling in both directions – when the two drill-holes met in 1905, they were only two centimetres out of alignment. In those days, that was a fantastic achievement.

While it ⁵ <u>was being built</u>, about 3,000 people worked on the construction every day. The working conditions weren't very good – for example, it was often very hot inside – and more than sixty people died ⁶ <u>while</u> the building of the tunnel.

The tunnel joins Switzerland and Italy, ⁷ <u>and</u> it has helped to make ⁸ <u>…</u> travel between the two countries a lot easier ⁹ <u>then</u> it was before. Now, people can put their car on the train and take it through the tunnel, and so they don't have to drive over the Simplon Pass.

I think this was a great thing to build all those years ago and it has made a big difference to the ¹⁰ <u>whole</u> of that part of Europe.

CAMBRIDGE ENGLISH: First

THiNK EXAMS

READING AND USE OF ENGLISH
Part 2: Open cloze

Workbook page 71

1 For questions 1–8, read the text below and think of the word which best fits each gap. Use only one word in each gap. There is an example at the beginning (0).

Reasons to be cheerful

Despite ⁰ _what_ you may hear on the news, the future is looking bright for teenagers. According to a government report, the economy is ¹_____ the point of making a dramatic recovery. And ²_____ the report is correct, those who will benefit most are the young. In fact, it predicts that ³_____ the time today's thirteen-year-olds leave school, unemployment will ⁴_____ fallen to an all-time low. The report, which was carried ⁵_____ by a leading employment agency, predicts that this growth will principally be in IT technology. It strongly recommends ⁶_____ increase in the funding of science and technology and points out that failure to do this will mean that the UK will fall behind its competitors. The message is clear: as ⁷_____ as the country continues to take education seriously, tomorrow's school leavers ⁸_____ enjoy a prosperous future.

SPEAKING
Part 2: Individual long turn

Workbook page 79

2 Here are two photographs. They show different ways of making lists. Compare the photographs, and say what the differences are and what you think are the main advantages of making lists in these ways.

TEST YOURSELF

UNITS 7 & 8

VOCABULARY

1 Complete the sentences with the words in the list. There are four extra words.

about | flourishes | down | worried | up | dread | forward
as long as | through | worked | point | succession | unless | on

1. John had lots of problems, but he didn't let them get him _____ . He stayed cheerful.
2. Sally is excited. She's _____ to go paragliding for the first time.
3. When we were planning the trip, Leo came _____ with some good ideas.
4. Mum said we couldn't go to the concert _____ we got a taxi home, because it'd be late.
5. He seems so down all the time. I'm really _____ about him.
6. My aunt is a great gardener. Everything she plants _____ .
7. The police are investigating a _____ of Post Office robberies.
8. The organisers wanted to run _____ the arrangements for the president's visit again.
9. I'm tired. I'm really looking _____ to the holidays.
10. Kate was on the _____ of leaving the house when Mr Hill phoned to cancel the meeting.

/10

GRAMMAR

2 Complete the sentences with the words in the list. There are two extra words.

won't | would be | would have | are going | will have | will | will be | don't

1. If Jenny had accepted the job offer, she _____ living in New York now.
2. By the end of the festival I _____ seen about fifteen films.
3. Watch out! You _____ to hit that cyclist!
4. Don't stay on the computer all night, or you _____ feel exhausted the next day.
5. If I were taller, I _____ been chosen for the basketball team.
6. While my parents are away on holiday I _____ looking after the dog.

3 Find and correct the mistake in each sentence.

1. It's Diana's birthday next Friday and she will have a party on Saturday.
2. I would have been happy if he would have come.
3. If I hadn't made so many mistakes, I would win the tennis match.
4. This time tomorrow, I'm lying on a beach in the sun.
5. If I had been taller, I wouldn't need the ladder.
6. We must finish cleaning the kitchen before our parents are arriving.

/12

FUNCTIONAL LANGUAGE

4 Choose the correct options.

1. A Oh dear, I have *no / every* chance of saving enough money to fly to Mexico.
   B Come on, look on the *better / bright* side. If you don't, you can buy that new phone you want.
2. A Yes, you can use my computer *unless / provided* you finish before six o'clock.
   B That's fine! There's *any / a good* chance I'll only need it for half an hour.
3. A Mum won't let me watch the match *unless / as long as* I tidy my room first.
   B Oh, *cheer / hang* up. Tidying your room won't take long – I'll help you!
4. A Yes, you can borrow my video camera *if / as long* I can use your computer for a couple of hours.
   B OK, *as long / provided* as you don't spill anything on it.

/8

MY SCORE /30

22 – 30
10 – 21
0 – 9

83

PRONUNCIATION

UNIT 5

The schwa sound

1 🔊 1.29 Read and listen to a voicemail message, paying attention to the words in blue. Which sound do they all share?

Thank you for calling **the** Computer Now Helpline. **To** find out how **to** zip **a** file, upgrade **a** system **or** stream **a** video, press 1. **To** learn how **to** connect **to** wifi, browse **the** Internet or post **an** update, press 2. For all other enquiries, press 3.

2 🔊 1.30 Listen, repeat and practise.

UNIT 6

Linking words with /dʒ/ and /tʃ/

1 🔊 1.33 Read and listen to the dialogue.

JACK <u>Would you</u> like a cup of tea?
SALLY <u>Do you</u> know what? I'd really prefer coffee.
JACK Oh! <u>Did you</u> buy some when you went out?
SALLY No. <u>Didn't you</u>?
JACK <u>Don't you</u> remember? I <u>told you</u> we didn't have any coffee!
SALLY <u>Do you</u> know what? Tea sounds great!

2 🔊 1.34 Listen, repeat and practise.

UNIT 7

Intonation: encouraging someone

1 🔊 2.05 Read and listen to the dialogue.

BECKY Hi, Harry! You don't look very happy. What's up?
HARRY Well… I just failed my driving test.
BECKY Oh! That's too bad… but **don't let it get you down**. Plenty of people fail the first time!
HARRY Actually, it's not the first time.
BECKY Oh well, **look on the bright side** – you can only get better!
HARRY I suppose so… I just feel kind of stupid.
BECKY **It'll be all right!** You just need a bit more practice, that's all. **I know you can do it!**

2 🔊 2.05 Draw arrows above the blue phrases to show how Becky's voice goes up and down.

3 🔊 2.06 Listen, repeat and practise.

UNIT 8

Weak forms with conditionals

1 🔊 2.11 Read and listen to the dialogue.

KIM Oh no! I forgot Mum's birthday! I <u>would've remembered</u> if I didn't have all these exams!
NELLIE Really, Kim… you <u>could've written</u> it in your diary.
KIM I <u>could've done</u> many things, Nellie. But that's not the point.
NELLIE You <u>should've asked</u> your dad to remind you! What are you going to do?

2 🔊 2.11 Listen again and (circle) the word in blue in which the /v/ sound in 've *is* pronounced. Why do you think this might be?

3 🔊 2.12 Listen, repeat and practise.

GET IT RIGHT!

UNIT 5
should

> **Learners often use *would* and *must* instead of *should*.**
>
> ✓ Lots of people think that animals **should** be free.
> ✗ Lots of people think that animals ~~must~~ be free.

For each pair of sentences tick the correct one.

1. a ☐ Your computer is very slow. I think you should upgrade your system.
   b ☐ Your computer is very slow. I think you must upgrade your system.
2. a ☐ Sally wouldn't have emigrated if she hadn't been unhappy here.
   b ☐ Sally shouldn't have emigrated if she hadn't been unhappy here.
3. a ☐ Our teachers should motivate us to study more so we do better in exams.
   b ☐ Our teachers would motivate us to study more so we do better in exams.
4. a ☐ We should launch the new product before the end of the month or we won't hit the sales figures. We've no option.
   b ☐ We must launch the new product before the end of the month or we won't hit the sales figures. We've no option.

UNIT 6
Comparatives

> **Learners often use the comparative instead of the superlative and vice versa.**
>
> ✓ That was the **worst** evening of my holiday.
> ✗ That was the ~~worse~~ evening of my holiday.
> ✓ Their behaviour seems to getting **worse**.
> ✗ Their behaviour seems to getting ~~worst~~.

Complete the sentences with the correct superlative or comparative in the list.

happier | happiest | harder | hardest
higher | highest | better | best

1. The _____ the questions, the more money can be won by the participants.
2. What's the _____ way to ask someone out?
3. When Liz got married it was the _____ day of her life.
4. The _____ the salary, the more extra money to spend you have.
5. The exam I sat yesterday was the _____ one I've ever done.
6. Luke and Sally's engagement party would have been _____ if they'd invited more people.
7. Tom decided to climb the _____ mountain in Scotland.
8. Some people think that the richer you are the _____ you are.

Linkers of contrast

> **Learners often confuse linkers or make mistakes with form.**
>
> ✓ **Although** I studied a lot I failed the exam.
> ✗ ~~Despite~~ I studied a lot I failed the exam.

Rewrite the sentences either by using a different linker or by changing the form of the sentence.

0. In spite they got engaged, they never got married.
   Although they got engaged, they never got married.
   In spite of getting engaged, they never got married.
1. Even though confessing to the crime, the police didn't arrest her.
2. We made an enquiry about the delivery. Despite, no one got back to us.
3. Nevertheless the fact that they made a complaint about the food, the chef didn't apologise.
4. The children took the move to the countryside in their stride, despite they had been happy living in the town.

UNIT 7
Future continuous

> **Learners often use the present continuous when the future continuous is more commonly used.**
>
> ✓ On holiday we **will be staying** in tents.
> ✗ On holiday we ~~are staying~~ in tents.

Tick the sentences which sound perfectly natural as they are and rewrite the other ones.

1 I'll see you tomorrow outside the hospital at 3 pm. ☐

2 I am seeing you sometime over the weekend, so I'll show you then. ☐

3 When we meet I'll be wearing a black dress and a hat. ☐

4 I'll come to the airport to pick you up. I'm waiting for you at arrivals. ☐

5 John won't come to the party on Saturday as he's busy. ☐

6 This time next week they will lie on a beach relaxing. ☐

UNIT 8
would

> **Learners often use *would* in the *if* clause of conditional sentences instead of using a present, past simple or past perfect form.**
>
> ✓ Don't hesitate to contact me if you **need** any more information.
> ✗ Don't hesitate to contact me if you ~~would~~ need any more information.
>
> ✓ If you **had come** to the park, you would have enjoyed yourself.
> ✗ If you ~~would have~~ come to the park, you would have enjoyed yourself.

Put the words in order to make sentences. In each sentence there is an extra word that you don't need.

1 If / would / run through / the / mistake / calculations / they / they / would / have / realised / had / their /.
_____

2 cook book / The / wouldn't / meal / wouldn't / turned out / lent / so well / if / you / hadn't / me / have / your /.
_____

3 would / 'll / that / She / do / her / provided / we / help / it /.
_____

4 get / infection / you / hands, / might / don't / would / wash / If / your / you / an /.
_____

5 The / wouldn't / been / have / ripped / would / it / had / cloth / if / stronger /.
_____

6 as / time / won't / It / problem / long / a / as / would / arrive / on / be / you /.
_____

STUDENTS A & C

UNIT 6, PAGE 56

Student A
You are an 18-year-old student who suffers from claustrophobia (which means you really don't like enclosed spaces). You can be in a lift for three or four minutes, but after that you panic and need to get out as soon as possible. When you are stressed, you usually sing to help you relax.

Student C
You are a middle-aged lawyer. You have work to do in your office and you think it's very important that you get to your office soon. You are not a very patient person. You do not like students or unemployed people very much, and you absolutely hate music.

STUDENTS B & D

UNIT 6, PAGE 56

Student B
You are an elderly person, about 65 years old. You have been in situations like this before and it doesn't worry you very much. However, you have an important appointment with your doctor in an hour's time so you really need to get out as soon as possible. You would like the other people to do something practical to fix the situation.

Student D
You are an unemployed person in your 20s. You are in the lift because you are going to a job interview which starts in 30 minutes. But it's not a job you really want so you are not very worried and you're relieved to have the excuse not to go. Also you are a very calm person and you enjoy helping other people. You also enjoy singing.

WORKBOOK 4B B2

Herbert Puchta, Jeff Stranks & Peter Lewis-Jones

CONTENTS

UNIT 5 Screen time	46
Grammar	46
Vocabulary	48
Reading	50
Writing	51
Listening	52
Exam practice: First	53

UNIT 6 Bringing people together	54
Grammar	54
Vocabulary	56
Reading	58
Writing	59
Listening	60
Exam practice: First	61
Consolidation 5 & 6	**62**

UNIT 7 Always look on the bright side	64
Grammar	64
Vocabulary	66
Reading	68
Writing	69
Listening	70
Exam practice: First	71

UNIT 8 Making lists	72
Grammar	72
Vocabulary	74
Reading	76
Writing	77
Listening	78
Exam practice: First	79
Consolidation 7 & 8	**80**

Pronunciation   page 119   **Grammar reference**   page 124
Irregular verb list   page 128

5 SCREEN TIME

GRAMMAR

Obligation, permission and prohibition (review) SB page 50

1 ★☆☆ **Circle the correct verbs to complete the sentences.**

1 You *don't have to / aren't supposed to* eat too many sweet things. They're bad for your teeth.
2 He *didn't let me / didn't need to* buy a new tablet. He already had one.
3 We *are not allowed to / had better* eat in the library. It's not permitted.
4 My parents *don't let me / allow me to* use my computer after 8 pm. They don't want me to spend all evening on it.
5 We *have to / don't have to* turn off our phones in school. We can't use them in class.
6 You *had better / shouldn't* spend all evening texting your friends. Do something else instead.

2 ★★☆ **Complete the sentences with the modal verbs in the list.**

aren't allowed to | had better | mustn't
didn't have to | made | didn't let

1 'You have to wear a hat and scarf today. It's cold.'
  My mum _____ me wear a hat and scarf today.
2 'You have to get to school early tomorrow. The coach leaves at 8 am.'
  I _____ be late to school tomorrow morning.
3 'You can't bring your dog into this restaurant.'
  We _____ take our dog into the restaurant.
4 'I really need a new school jumper. This one is too small.'
  I _____ buy a new jumper.
5 'You can't go to the cinema tonight.'
  My dad _____ us go to the cinema last night.
6 'It wasn't necessary for Tom to lend me his tablet.'
  Tom _____ lend me his tablet.

3 ★★★ **Unscramble the sentences to complete the dialogues. Use the correct form of the verbs.**

1 A Why haven't you got your mobile phone with you today?
  B mum / My / make / it / leave / me / at / home
  _____

2 A Why didn't you come climbing on Saturday?
  B parents / My / not allow / to / me / go
  _____

3 A Are you ready to go yet?
  B No, I can't find my Geography homework.
  A had better / You / find / it / soon
  _____
  The class has already started.

4 A Why were you late yesterday?
  B have to / I / my / Sorry, / bedroom / tidy
  _____

5 A I gave Joanna my phone yesterday.
  B must not / you / But / give / phone / your / anyone / to
  _____

6 A Did you see the match last night?
  B stay / it / parents / No, / up / not let / my / me / for
  _____

4 ★★★ **Complete the sentences so that they are true for you. Choose from the verbs in the list and give a reason.**

must / mustn't | let / don't let
have to / don't have to | should / shouldn't
allowed to / not allowed to

1 My parents _____ me play on the tablet as much as I want because _____
2 I _____ use my mobile phone too much because _____
3 I _____ have a TV in my bedroom because _____
4 I _____ think carefully before I post photos of friends and family because _____

5 SCREEN TIME

Necessity: (didn't) need to / needn't have SB page 51

5 ★ ☆ ☆ Match the statements and responses.

1 The battery for my laptop has run out. ☐
2 I don't have enough space on my hard drive. ☐
3 I didn't have a European plug. ☐
4 We were late yesterday. ☐
5 I arrived an hour before the concert. ☐
6 I bought a Spanish dictionary yesterday. ☐
7 I failed my History exam. ☐
8 My friends keep texting me. I can't work. ☐

a You needn't have left home so early.
b You needed to take an earlier bus.
c I've got one. You needn't have bought one.
d You need to get a charger.
e Turn your phone off. You need to finish your homework.
f You needed to do more revision for it.
g You needed to get an adaptor.
h You need to delete some files.

6 ★★ ☆ Read the situations. Then make comments with *didn't need to* or *needn't have*.

0 I bought two concert tickets. My friend had already bought them.
   I needn't have bought the tickets.

1 Daniel didn't do his homework last night. He'd already done it the night before.

2 Sally didn't revise for her History exam. She passed it easily anyway.

3 I took a thick jumper with me yesterday but it was a hot, sunny day.

4 Lucy cooked Brian a birthday cake but his mum had already bought him one from the shops.

5 Liam didn't have dinner at home because he knew there was food at the party.

6 We took a taxi from the station but the hotel was only 200 metres away so we could have walked there.

7 I'd already sent Lara a text and that's why I didn't call her.

Ability in the past: could, was / were able to, managed to, succeeded in doing SB page 53

7 ★★ ☆ Write sentences using the prompts.

0 I / not manage / mend / my phone / yet
   I haven't managed to mend my phone yet.

1 James / not succeed / pass / his driving test / yet

2 I / not able to / find / my charger / yet

3 Sarah / not able to / swim / yesterday

4 We / succeed / climb / Ben Nevis / at the weekend

5 They / not able to / access / the Internet / at / the hotel / last night

6 He / not have / much / time / but / he / manage to / finish / the project

GET IT RIGHT!

must

Learners often use *should*, *would*, and *can* instead of *must*.

✓ I **mustn't** forget to give you my phone number.
✗ I ~~shouldn't~~ forget to give you my phone number.

Choose the correct verb to complete the sentences.

1 We *can / must / would* admit that peer pressure can be a problem.
2 They *shouldn't / can't / mustn't* be using artificial flowers – it doesn't look nice.
3 I really *can / would / must* get a new headset; this one doesn't work very well.
4 Harry *mustn't / can't / wouldn't* have arrived yet as his car isn't here.
5 To get this job applicants *can / should / must* be proficient speakers in Chinese. Non-Chinese speakers won't be considered.
6 *Should / Would / Must* you do that? It's highly irritating!
7 The children *wouldn't / mustn't / can't* arrive home late unless there was a problem.
8 The spectators *should / must / can* have seen the man run on stage. He ran right across it!

VOCABULARY

Word list

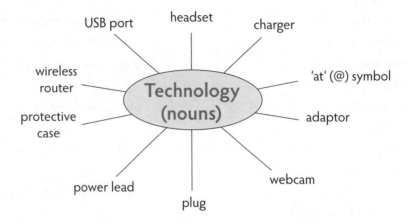

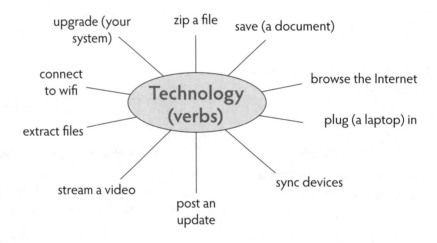

Key words in context

artificial	They're not real flowers. They're **artificial**. Look! They're plastic.
decade	In the last **decade**, technology has changed dramatically. I wonder what new technologies we'll see in the next ten years.
emigrate	Every year, thousands of people **emigrate** to another country.
excessive	Five hours a day online is an **excessive** amount of time. I'm not allowed to spend more than two hours.
influence	Max's performance of Dracula in the school play was **influenced** by Christopher Lee. Max has watched all the Christopher Lee films and he is a big fan.
launch	Facebook's website was **launched** on 4th February 2004.
motivate	My dad is a keen footballer and that **motivated** me to join my local football club.
peer pressure	There is **peer pressure** at school to have the latest smartphone.
proficient	My granddad is a **proficient** Internet user. He can do everything on the Internet now.

5 SCREEN TIME

Technology (nouns) SB page 50

1 ★☆☆ Unscramble the words and match them to the pictures.

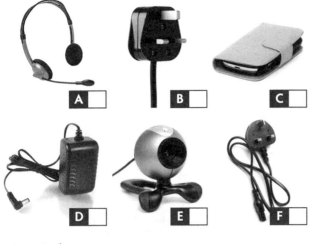

1 vetecitpro seac _____
2 ewmabc _____
3 gcerahr _____
4 woper dela _____
5 glup _____
6 dehates _____

2 ★★☆ What do they need? Match the sentences (1–4) to (a–d).

1 *I'm connecting my camera to my laptop.* ☐
2 *You need to include it in your email address.* ☐
3 *What do I need to connect to the wifi?* ☐
4 *You can't use a European plug here.* ☐

a wireless router   c USB port
b adaptor   d 'at' symbol

3 ★★☆ Read the definitions. What are they?

1 It provides access to the Internet or to a private computer network. _____
2 It stops my phone from being scratched or damaged. _____
3 It connects my laptop to the mains electricity. _____
4 It holds an earphone and a microphone in place on your head. _____
5 You can use it to video chat over the Internet. _____

Technology (verbs) SB page 51

4 ★★☆ Read the clues and complete the puzzle with the missing verbs.

1 We … interviews with our favourite singers.
2 My sister … updates on her blog once a week.
3 When I want to email big files, I always … them.
4 I'd better … my laptop in before the battery dies.
5 My dad usually … his phone every two years.
6 I need to learn how to … a file from a zipped folder.
7 I … all of my digital photos on my memory stick.
8 I want to … music from my laptop onto my phone.
9 You can find lots of interesting information when you … the Internet
10 If you go to the café on the High Street, you can … to the wifi for free.

5 ★★☆ Complete the dialogues with the correct form of the technology verbs.

zip | save | browse | connect | post | upgrade

1 A Have you _____ anything interesting on your blog this week?
  B No, I haven't had time.
2 A You've had the same phone for years. You should _____ it for a newer model.
  B I don't want to. I'm happy with this one.
3 A You look tired.
  B I am. I _____ the Internet for hours last night.
4 A I've got no space left on my hard drive.
  B You should _____ some of the large files. That will free up some space.
5 A How do I _____ my games console to the Internet?
  B You need access to a wireless connection.
6 A There isn't enough space to _____ all my music and photos on my hard drive.
  B You should store them on a cloud server.

Pronunciation
The schwa sound
Go to page 119.

READING

1 REMEMBER AND CHECK Answer the questions. Then check your answers in the texts on page 49 in the Student's Book.

1. What happens when parents try to limit the amount of time their children spend in front of a screen?
2. When did screen time first become an issue?
3. Which city doesn't allow large outdoor advertising any more?
4. What percentage of the population said the ban had improved their quality of life?
5. Give three examples that the text says we use our mobiles for other than making and receiving calls.
6. What have people lost the ability to do?

2 Read the article quickly. What do these numbers refer to?

1. 234
2. 2006
3. 4.7 million

The Digital Black Hole

Libraries around the world still hold copies of books printed hundreds of years ago. Will e-books still be accessible to us in hundreds of years' time? Librarians are worried that digital information and digital books are already being lost. Technology is always changing, and even now, we cannot access information typed in programs we used ten or fifteen years ago. Is digital data in danger of disappearing into a digital black hole?

Amazingly, we still have copies of the first published collection of William Shakespeare's 36 plays, *The First Folio*. That's not bad for a book that's nearly 500 years old. The folio was published in 1623. Around 800 copies were printed and 234 known copies still survive today.

More amazingly, there are still copies of the 13th century scientist Al-Jazari's illustrated book on automation and robotics, *The Book of Knowledge of Ingenious Mechanical Devices*. It is thought that Al-Jazari finished writing his book on the 16th January 1206 in Mesopotamia (modern-day Turkey) and copies still survive today.

Books are quite easy to store. They hold a large amount of information in a small space. Most importantly, we don't need any special equipment to open them. But what about the documents stored on your computer now? Will people be able to read them in 800, 500 or even 10 years' time?

Technology moves fast. Documents we saved on floppy discs ten or twenty years ago can't be accessed now. We can't open them on our 21st century laptops. What about all your digital photographs? Every second, thousands of them are uploaded to social media. There is no physical copy. What will happen to them? Will they be lost in a few years' time? Now you save them in .jpg or .tiff format. In ten years' time, there will be another format and another program to open your photos with. This new program will not be able to open your old .jpg or .tiff files. People have recognised this problem and there are now online retailers who will print physical photo albums of your Facebook posts.

Music is in danger of being lost too. We have to think of new ways to store it. The increasing disappearance of the technology to play tapes, vinyl records and even CDs means that millions of music recordings and songs could be lost forever. Archivists must copy this music or find the best way of preserving it for future generations.

When a website closes down, all the information on that website is deleted. It's gone forever. It has disappeared into the 'digital black hole'. Organisations have understood this issue. In 2004, the British Library in the UK started to archive websites that are important culturally and academically for future generations, just like paper-based literature. In 2010, the US Library of Congress signed an agreement with Twitter to archive public Tweets sent by Americans. They have archived all public Tweets sent since the start of Twitter in 2006. That's 400 million Tweets every day!

Wikipedia, the online encyclopedia, holds more than 4.7 million articles. It is the result of over 100 million hours of work. In the event of a digital catastrophe, it could all disappear. The only solution is to print it all out and keep physical copies. In 2014, Pediapress launched a crowdfunding scheme with the aim of raising $50,000 to print Wikipedia as 1,000 books of 1,200 pages each.

With all the amazing new digital technology available to us today, we still have to rely on the centuries-old technology of printing. For now, it seems printed copies are still the safest way to store information.

3 Read the article again and complete the sentences. Use between 1 and 2 words.

1. Shakespeare's *First Folio* was published in _____ .
2. Al-Jazari's book about automation and robotics was written at the beginning of the _____ century in _____ .
3. You don't have to have any _____ to open a book.
4. In order to solve the problem of losing your digital photos, you should _____ physical copies of them.
5. We must _____ and public Tweets for future generations.
6. Even though we have lots of amazing new technology, _____ are still the most secure way to save information.

5 SCREEN TIME

DEVELOPING WRITING

A guide to buying a phone

1 Read Jamie's guide to buying a phone. Circle three things that are important to him.

A the ringtones   B the battery life   C the pen   D the camera   E the games

---

My Instruction Guide to Buying a New Phone

What do you look for when you buy a phone? Does your phone have to be the latest model? Does it have to look good or do you just want a phone that's easy to use and small enough to fit in your pocket? Before you buy your new phone, decide what's important to you.

First I look at the battery life of a phone. That's very important to me. It must have a long battery life. It mustn't ever go flat on me. Next I look at the camera quality. I like taking photos so I have to have a phone with a good camera. I also like to have a phone with a big screen so I can see the photos clearly. Then I look at how easy it is to do things, for example adding a name to my contacts, finding someone in my contacts, sending a text message to multiple people, using the autocorrect and sending a photo. After that I check the games. What are they like? Finally, I look at the price of the phone. Is it affordable? I do that last but my mum says I should do it first!

Everyone has different priorities when buying a phone, but these are the things that are important to me.

---

2 Read Jamie's guide again and underline the sequencing words. Then complete the list of sequencing words.

First

_____

Then

_____

Finally

3 You are going to write your own guide to buying (a) a new phone or (b) a tablet or (c) a laptop. First brainstorm your ideas and complete the mind map.

4 Now pick five of those ideas and write them in sequence using the terms below.

First

Next

Then

After that

Finally

5 Now write your own guide to buying a new phone, tablet or laptop in 200–250 words.

CHECKLIST

- [ ] Include modal verbs in your guide
- [ ] Include a variety of useful technology nouns and verbs
- [ ] The information in your guide is in a logical order (the most important feature first, the least important last)
- [ ] Use sequencing words

LISTENING

1 🔊 17 Listen to the conversation between Matt, Alicia and Oscar and circle the correct option.

1 Alicia spends a lot of time playing *tennis* / *video games*.
2 Alicia *texts* / *sees* her friends all the time.
3 When Jo called Matt, she was *excited* / *upset*.

2 🔊 17 Listen again and answer the questions.

1 What do Matt, Alicia and Oscar have to do for homework?
   _____
2 Why doesn't Alicia want to let her mum see their homework?
   _____
3 What should Alicia stop doing?
   _____
4 What does Oscar suggest Alicia should do?
   _____
5 What is Alicia looking forward to hearing about?
   _____
6 Why was Jo upset?
   _____

3 🔊 17 Listen again and complete these parts of the conversation.

1 MATT   What do you think of the homework? I can't believe Mr Harrow _____ this thing.
   ALICIA You mean the video gaming guide for parents? I think it's OK. Mind you, I'm not going to show it to my mum. She's already worried about me spending too much time playing video games. She _____ during the week at all.
   OSCAR You do spend a lot of time on the games console, Alicia. You _____ more.
2 ALICIA What do you mean?
   MATT   You know what he means. You just sit around staring at screens all day.
   OSCAR You're turning into a couch potato. You _____ some exercise.
3 JO   Hi, Alicia. I haven't heard from you for ages.
   ALICIA I know, I'm sorry. Listen. Matt, Oscar and I are going to Bob's Café. Would you like to come along? We can't wait to hear about your skiing trip.
   JO   I'd love to come. I'll meet you all there in an hour.
   ALICIA Great. We'll see you there. Oh, and you _____ any money – it's on me!

DIALOGUE

1 Complete the dialogues with the phrases in the list.

need to finish | had better get | made me
have to help me | should leave | make me do it

1
MARIA Hi, Susie. How did your audition go yesterday?
SUSIE I don't think I'll get a part in the school play.
MARIA How come?
SUSIE I made a mess of the audition. I couldn't remember my lines. It was awful. Then they _____ sing. And that was worse. You know I can't sing in tune.

2
JAKE You _____ with the washing up, Sarah. Mum told you to.
SARAH I can't. I'm busy. I _____ this essay.
JAKE You're always busy. You never do anything around the house.
SARAH Oh, no. Here we go.
JAKE You're always on your phone or on your laptop. I always have to do the washing up. It's not fair.
SARAH You can't _____ , Jake.
JAKE No, I can't, but Mum can and she's just come home now.

3
ANTONIO What's the matter with you?
JOE I'm just tired. That's all.
ANTONIO Why are you so tired?
JOE I'm not sure. Mind you, I did go to sleep really late last night. I started browsing the Internet and I couldn't stop.
ANTONIO That explains it then. You _____ some sleep now. And you _____ your phone in the living room at night. If it's not in your bedroom, you won't be able to go online. Problem solved.

2 Now write a dialogue of between six and eight lines. Complain to a friend that he/she is spending too much time in front of a screen. Give him/her some advice. Include some of the words below.

should / shouldn't | need to | let | make
have to / don't have to | must / mustn't | had better

CAMBRIDGE ENGLISH: First

Reading and Use of English part 7

> ### Exam guide: multiple matching
> In this part of the exam you have to read a text or four short texts. Then you must match a prompt to the texts/parts of the text. This is a test of your understanding of the text.
> - Read each text carefully to get an overall understanding before you answer the questions.
> - Make sure you read the titles too because they may help you find the answers.
> - Look for words with a similar or the same meaning in the texts and the questions.
> - Check for words with a positive or negative meaning.

1 You are going to read an advertisement for four different tech courses. For questions 1–10, choose from the courses (A–D). The courses may be chosen more than once.

On this course …
1. you have to work with a small group of people.
2. the main focus will be Hypertext Markup Language.
3. you have to have some artistic and creative ability.
4. you will learn the necessary skills to get a job with a digital company.
5. you will learn the basics of web development.
6. the first thing you do is learn to draw on a computer.
7. you must face new challenges each day.
8. there is time away from the screens to participate in activities outside.
9. you will leave with the skills to develop you own web pages.
10. there will be competitions so students can test their skills.

Tech Heaven
Courses for the digital age

Course A: Animation
This course is for creative people who like to draw. You don't have to have amazing drawing skills but you need to have some artistic talent. You start learning how to draw on the computer and you finish by making interactive films. You work very closely with teachers to learn the essential techniques. You choose to do either game design or an animation. There is a huge gaming library at the camp so you will have the opportunity to test your gaming skills against other students in our gaming tournaments.

Course B: Web
This course is for teens who want to create their own web pages and websites. On this course, you will learn the foundations of web development. The primary focus of the course is HTML, which makes up the building blocks of the Internet. You will leave the camp with your own web page and you will be able to go home and create other web pages.

Course C: Coding
This course is ideal for students with some programming experience who want to improve their coding skills. Most devices, programs, computers and robots run on software applications so you must have programming, scripting and coding skills to get a job with a digital company. You will learn from experienced and supportive staff and you will leave the school equipped with the basic skills. There are two hours of outdoor sports activities a day to get some fresh air.

Course D: Robotics
This course is all about robots. You will work in small teams and learn how to use VEX® Robotics Design System. You'll build a robot that will compete in robo-football and obstacle courses. You will learn how to build robotic arms and advanced sensors. Every day will present you with a new challenge and every day will be more fun and more inspiring than the last.

6 BRINGING PEOPLE TOGETHER

GRAMMAR
Comparatives SB page 58

1 ★☆☆ Look at the website and mark the sentences T (true) or F (false).

www.travelcompare.com – London – Paris	JOURNEY TIME	PRICE	COMFORT	FREQUENCY	NUMBER OF PASSENGERS PER WEEK	OVERALL EXPERIENCE
Euroair	50m	£350	*****	Mon, Tues and Fri	200	*****
Budgetline	1h 15m	£21	*	Wed, Fri and Sat	200	*

1 Euroair is not nearly as quick as Budgetline. ☐
2 Budgetline is far more frequent than Euroair. ☐
3 Budgetline is not nearly as good as Euroair. ☐
4 Budgetline is much cheaper than Euroair. ☐
5 Euroair is much more unpopular than Budgetline. ☐
6 Budgetline is a lot slower than Euroair. ☐
7 Euroair is much better than Budgetline. ☐
8 Budgetline is nowhere near as expensive as Euroair. ☐

2 ★★★ Look at the website in Exercise 1 again and use the words in brackets to make sentences about the London to Paris flights.

0 (nowhere near / comfortable)
   Budgetline is nowhere near as comfortable as Euroair.

1 (much / expensive)

2 (just as / popular)

3 (far / quick)

4 (nowhere near / good)

5 (just as / frequent)

6 (not nearly / cheap)

3 ★★☆ Use a ' … and …' expression and the adjective in brackets to rewrite each sentence.

0 The boys just won't stop growing. (tall)
   The boys are growing taller and taller.

1 Every year there are more cars on the road. (busy)

2 I love spring. Every day the sun stays up a few minutes later. (long)

3 Scientists say the temperature of the Earth is increasing. (hot)

4 The price of food is increasing by the week. (expensive)

4 ★★★ Use a 'the …, the …' comparative expression to rewrite each sentence.

0 Loud music gives me a bad headache.
   The louder the music gets, the worse my headache gets.

1 Hot weather makes me angry.

2 Driving fast is dangerous.

3 When you're hungry, food tastes better.

4 Old people need less sleep.

6 BRINGING PEOPLE TOGETHER

Linkers of contrast SB page 61

5 ★☆☆ Match the sentence halves.

1. Although not many people came to the party,
2. I feel really tired today
3. Liam invited Dan to his party
4. In spite of having sold millions of books,
5. The film was in French so I didn't understand much.
6. The athlete wasn't 100% fit.

a. even though they're not the best of friends.
b. no one knows who she is.
c. However, I still really enjoyed it.
d. Nevertheless, she still won the race easily.
e. we still had a great time.
f. despite having had a really good night's sleep.

6 ★★☆ Complete the card with the missing linkers.

¹A _ _ ou _ _ you annoy me at least once a day.
²I _ _ i _ e o _ the fact you always get your way.
³E _ e _ _ _ ou _ _ you take things without saying 'please'.
And ⁴ _ e _ i _ e the mess in my room that you leave.
It seems I don't like you.
⁵ _ e _ e _ _ _ e _ _ , that's not true.
There's something I need to say about you.
It seems we're so different. ⁶ _ o _ e _ e _ , we're not.
You are my sister – the best friend that I've got.

7 ★★★ Combine the two sentences using the word in brackets.

Unusual facts about me

0. I'm short. I'm good at basketball. (despite)
   Despite being short, I'm good at basketball.

1. I've got two bikes. I can't ride a bike. (although)
   _____

2. My mum's French. I don't speak French. (however)
   _____

3. I love Italian food. I don't like pizza. (even though)
   _____

4. I always go to bed early. I'm always late for school. (nevertheless)
   _____

5. I'm 1.75m tall. I'm only 14. (in spite of)
   _____

GET IT RIGHT!

however

Learners often use *however* incorrectly.

✓ I looked back in his direction. **However**, he had vanished.

✗ I looked back in his direction ~~however~~, he had vanished.

Match the sentences, then rewrite them using *however*.

0. Tom asked Helen out. — *a*
   Tom asked Helen out. However, she said no.

1. Ethan was offered the position of school counsellor.

2. Loom bands used to be a big craze.

3. The passengers were stuck on the train for two hours.

4. The Ice Bucket Challenge raised awareness about ALS.

5. President Obama refused to do the challenge.

a. She said no.
b. Nobody spoke to each other.
c. He turned it down.
d. He donated money instead.
e. It also wasted a lot of water.
f. It seems to be over now.

VOCABULARY

Word list

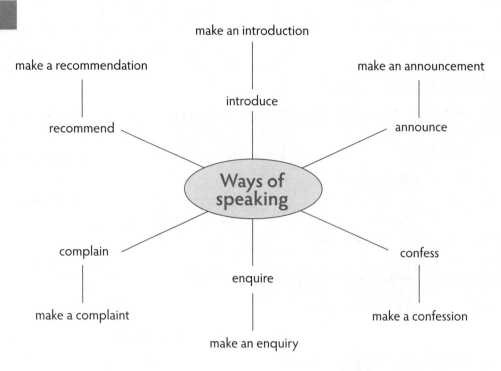

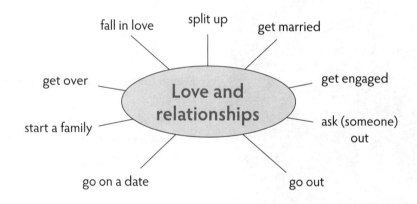

Key words in context

craze	In 2014 loom bands were a huge **craze** all over the planet.
dreaded	My **dreaded** piano exam is next week. I'm not looking forward to it at all.
go viral	The video of his cat playing the piano **went viral**. People were watching it all over the world.
groan	The children **groaned** when the teacher told them he was giving them a surprise test.
in their stride	When the plane was delayed by 4 hours most people took it **in their stride** and didn't complain (though of course a few were unhappy).
nominate	I'd like to **nominate** Luca for class president.
participant	The **participants** in this quiz show can win up to £100,000.
sufferer	Doctors say there will soon be a new medicine to help allergy **sufferers**.
sweep	Every year dozens of hurricanes **sweep** through the area.

6 BRINGING PEOPLE TOGETHER

Ways of speaking (SB page 58)

1 ★☆☆ Unscramble the verbs and then match them to the nouns.

verb
1 edomrcnme _____
2 nosecfs _____
3 toridnceu _____
4 reuqeni _____
5 nnoanuec _____
6 icmnlaop _____

noun (to make a/an …)
a enquiry
b confession
c announcement
d complaint
e recommendation
f introduction

2 ★★☆ Circle the correct option.

1 'What time does the train leave?'
   Making a/an *confession / introduction / enquiry*
2 'This fish isn't cooked properly.'
   Making a/an *complaint / introduction / announcement*
3 'The library will close in half an hour.'
   Making a/an *confession / recommendation / announcement*
4 'You should try the pepperoni pizza. It's excellent.'
   Making a/an *enquiry / recommendation / complaint*
5 'Harry, I'd like you to meet Tom.'
   Making a/an *introduction / announcement / enquiry*
6 'I'm really sorry, it was me who broke the computer.'
   Making a *complaint / confession / recommendation*

3 ★★☆ Complete the sentences with the missing verbs.

1 'OK, it was me. I ate the last piece of cake,' she _____.
2 'Can you tell me what time the shop closes?' she _____.
3 'The Internet isn't working in my room,' she _____ to the hotel manager.
4 'You should read this book, it's great,' he _____.
5 He _____ me to Ian. 'Ian, this is Dan. Dan, this is Ian.'
6 'I've got a new job,' he _____ to the whole room.

Love and relationships (SB page 59)

4 ★☆☆ Circle the correct words.

1 Sometimes I think I'll never fall *on / in* love.
2 Have you heard? Deb and Dexter have *started / split* up.
3 We got *married / engaged* in a church.
4 Bob just proposed to me and I said 'yes'. I can't believe it. I'm *engaged / married*.
5 I really want to ask Jim *out / up* but I'm too scared.
6 Harry and Bella have been *going / asking* out together for half a year already.
7 My brother's going *on / off* a date tonight. He's so nervous.
8 They've only just got married so I don't think they'll want to *get / start* a family soon.
9 Liam is still in love with Jessica. I don't think he'll ever get *up with / over* her.

5 ★★☆ Put the events in order.

☐ He said 'yes' and they agreed to go on a date.
☐ Apparently they're already thinking of starting a family.
`1` Olivia split up with Mike.
☐ It didn't take them long to fall in love.
☐ They got married a few weeks ago.
☐ It took him a long time to get over it.
☐ And six months later they got engaged.
☐ Eventually Lucy, his friend's sister, asked him out.
☐ It was a success and they started going out together.

57

READING

1 REMEMBER AND CHECK Read the article on page 60 of the Student's Book again. Write down the significance of these numbers.

0 2014   *The year the ice-bucket challenge happened.*
1 $10   _____
2 $100   _____
3 24   _____
4 2   _____
5 2.5 million _____
6 150   _____
7 15%   _____
8 10%   _____

2 Read the two stories. Make a list of all the things they have got in common.

The kindness of strangers

When Katie Cutler heard about an attack on 67-year-old Alan Barnes, she immediately knew what she had to do, even though she had never met him.

Alan had been mugged outside his home in Gateshead in the North East of England. He had been pushed to the ground by a man demanding money, who then ran off after Alan cried for help. For Alan, who has problems with his eyesight and is only 1.37m tall, the attack was terrifying and he felt reluctant to return back home alone.

When the story made the news, Katie immediately set up a page on a fundraising website called *Go Fund Me* with the intention of making £500 to help Alan find a new house to rent. The story went viral on the Internet and was picked up by most TV news stations. Less than a week after the fund was started Katie had raised £284,000 with donations from 21,700 people. With people making donations from the UK, Canada, the Netherlands and other countries, it was truly an international response.

Alan had the chance to thank Katie in person when the two finally met. He told her that he planned to use the money to buy a home of his own and several local builders had also offered to help make sure that Alan's new house was in perfect condition, and what he deserved.

Glenn Buratti had a disappointing turnout for his birthday party to celebrate his 6th birthday. Despite having invited all the children from his class, not one of them turned up at his house in Florida, USA on the day.

Glenn, who suffers from mild autism and epilepsy, was so upset that his mother Ashley decided to share her frustration on Facebook. She posted a message in which she told of the situation and the sadness she felt seeing the disappointment of her son.

It wasn't long before the online community was in touch and within minutes many people had got in contact asking if they could bring their children over. But it wasn't just children who came, the news also reached the local sheriff's office, which sent a helicopter to fly over his house to the young boy's delight.

A few days later a surprised Glenn received a visit at home from the county police and fire services, who had come to wish him a happy birthday and gave the happy boy a tour of their many vehicles. Glenn also became an Internet star with his story going viral and being featured in newspapers and TV news stations all over the world.

3 Read the stories again. Who might have said these things (and to whom)?

	Who said it?	… to whom?
1 Why is there no one here?		
2 I can't wait to move.		
3 Look. The pilot's waving at you.		
4 When I started this I could never have imagined how generous people could be.		
5 Thank you. You've changed my life.		
6 Leave me alone.		
7 Why is there a fire engine outside our house?		
8 Why didn't you just tell me you weren't coming?		

4 Choose two of the characters from either story and write a short (8 line) dialogue between them.

DEVELOPING WRITING

An essay about charity

1. Read the essay question. Then read the essay and tick the correct summary of the writer's thoughts.

   ☐ She believes it's better to donate money.
   ☐ She believes it's better to donate time.
   ☐ She believes that all donations are welcome.

   > **It's better to donate your time than your money. What do you think?**

   When most people hear of a charity asking for a donation they probably wonder how much money they can give. But money's not the only thing you can donate – your time can be just as valuable.

   For example, my grandmother spends three afternoons a week volunteering in the local Oxfam shop. One of my friends' fathers spends Monday mornings driving elderly people to their hospital appointments for free. Then there are all those people who donate their lives to helping less fortunate people overseas, doctors and rescue workers who go out to help when earthquakes hit, for example. Of course, they get paid a little, but nowhere near as much as they could earn doing their jobs at home.

   If you've got spare money, then making a donation is not too much trouble. You simply drop some coins in a collection box, buy items from charity organisations or make online payments. It never takes more than a few minutes. Giving away your time for free is different and it shows real dedication to the charity.

   Charities rely on the kindness of people and without them, the good work that they do would not get done. Whether it be your time or your money, most charities are always happy to accept either.

Writing tip: using examples

- You can often make your essays more accessible to the reader by including some real examples from everyday life. This will help the reader relate more easily to what you are saying. For example, this essay is all about charitable donations, both of money and time. The reader has included examples of both.
  e.g: Time: grandmother helping in local charity shop.
  Money: put money in a collection box.

- This is not only a good chance to help you engage your reader, but it can also give you the chance to show your range of vocabulary. It will also help with your organisation too.

2. Look back at the essay and find two more examples from real life of:

   How people donate their time:
   _____
   _____

   How people donate their money:
   _____

3. Write down three more ways that people can donate their time to charity.

   1 _____
   2 _____
   3 _____

4. Now write your answer to the essay question in around 200 words.

CHECKLIST

☐ Include good examples from everyday life
☐ Make your opinion clear in the last paragraph
☐ Make sure you answer the question asked
☐ Try and show a good range of vocabulary

LISTENING

1 🔊 18 Listen to three conversations Ava has during her journey to Scotland. Order the pictures.

A

B

C

2 🔊 18 Listen again and answer the questions.

CONVERSATION 1

1 How much cheaper is the later train?
_____

2 What time train does Ava get?
_____

CONVERSATION 2

3 What three items does Ava choose?
_____

4 How much more expensive is a large juice?
_____

CONVERSATION 3

5 How long is Ava staying in Glasgow?
_____

6 How long is Ava staying on the Isle of Mull?
_____

3 🔊 18 Complete the sentences from the conversations, then listen again and check.

CONVERSATION 1

TICKET OFFICER	If you can wait an hour and get the 9.55 it's a w_____ l_____ cheaper.
AVA	Yes, that's a much better idea b_____ f_____ .

CONVERSATION 2

ASSISTANT	It's e_____ the best deal for you.
ASSISTANT	And it's e_____ cheaper if you've got a Trainclub card.

CONVERSATION 3

PASSENGER	Mull's f_____ and a_____ more spectacular than the Lake District.
PASSENGER	It's smaller and m_____ less crowded.

DIALOGUE

1 Put the dialogue in order.

	DAD	It's a ten minute walk!
	DAD	You know what? I've got a good idea. You drive the kids in the car, or taxi or whatever. I'll take the train and we'll all meet on the beach.
	DAD	No chance, I thought we'd make it a tech free day too. Just a good old family day out on the train.
	DAD	I thought we'd go to Prestatyn. It's by far a nicer beach.
1	DAD	Who fancies a day at the beach?
5	DAD	I said how about a beach day, not a shopping day. Tim, how about you?
	DAD	I'm not. It's a whole lot easier than taking the car. And the train's quicker too. It's easily the best option.
13	MUM	We'll probably miss the train and have to wait hours for the next one.
	MUM	That sounds like a great idea. Shall we go to Llandudno?
	MUM	Well, I'm not so sure. I think I agree with the kids on this one. It's miles more convenient to take the car. I mean we've got to get to the station…
	LUCY	But Llandudno's got better shops by far.
	LUCY	The train?! Please tell me you're joking.
9	TIM	Yeah, Dad. Please tell us you're joking.
	TIM	Can I take my tablet with me?
	TIM	It'd be even quicker if we took a taxi.

2 Imagine the family are on the beach. They are deciding where to eat lunch. Write a 10 line dialogue. Try and use some comparative structures.

Pronunciation

Linking words with /dʒ/ and /tʃ/
Go to page 119. 🔊

CAMBRIDGE ENGLISH: First

Reading and Use of English part 7

You are going to read an article about four teenagers talking about how they use social media. For questions 1–10, choose from the teenagers (A–D). The teenagers may be used more than once.

Which teenager …

1. likes to post photos on social media?
2. thinks it's more popular with the older generation?
3. has phases when they use social media more?
4. uses social media less than they did before?
5. gave up using social media because of a bad experience?
6. uses social media to let their friends know a lot of the things that are happening in their life?
7. likes to use social media for practical things?
8. doesn't think their life is interesting enough to write about it on social media?
9. thinks people hide their true emotions on social media?
10. uses social media to feel closer to friends they don't see every day?

A Gabby

I have a strange relationship with social media. I can go for months without using it and then I'll spend a week or so posting stuff on my wall every half an hour. Then someone will write something horrible on it and I'll stop using it again for a while. I think when I'm generally happy I don't feel the need to use it but when I'm not quite so happy it makes me feel better if I do use it. It's funny really, everyone on social media always seems so happy but I'm sure they aren't. They're probably just like me – pretending to be. I helped my mum set up an account the other day. It was funny to see how excited she got with this 'new' technology. Anyway, in a couple of days she had over 200 friends. I think she's more popular than me.

B Andy

I used to be a massive fan of social media but these days I don't use it nearly as much as I used to. To be honest, I think it's something that appeals more to old people like my parents. They think it's a brilliant way of getting back in touch with people they haven't seen for years. It's different to my situation. I see most of my friends every day so I don't really need it to keep in touch. I do use it, however, for organising things. I play football on Sunday mornings so every Saturday evening I send out a message to see who wants to play and to check if we've got enough players. It's really useful for that sort of thing. I also use it sometimes if I want to get in contact with just one person privately. It's good for that but I don't really feel the need to share my life online.

C Carmen

I never really use social media. It's not that I'm against it, it's just that I don't really have the time. I'm too busy with my day-to-day life, school work, piano lessons, dance classes. I just don't really have the time to sit down and let people know what's happening in my life and I'm sure they'd find it really boring if I did. Mine isn't the most exciting life. Besides, I see all my best friends every day so I can let them know what's happening face-to-face. It's a lot quicker. But I wasn't always like this. When I first got my phone about three years ago I used to spend hours updating my Facebook page, but then I started to get some nasty comments on my wall. They were pretty upsetting and I found the best way to stop this happening was to not use social media. To be honest I don't really miss it much.

D Mike

I love social media. I use it all the time. I must write at least eight posts a day on my wall. I've got friends in quite a few different places and I think it's the perfect way of keeping in touch with everyone and letting them know what's going on in my life – it doesn't have to just be the big things, I think it's important to share the small things too, like a good book you've read, a photo of a delicious meal and so on. I know some people think it's a bit silly to share so much of your life but I think if you've got good friends, they're interested in hearing these things. It's great to see their comments too. It makes you feel like you're actually with them and you don't miss them so much. I also message friends individually when I've got something more personal to say. But I don't do this so often.

CONSOLIDATION

LISTENING

1 🔊 20 **Listen to Sam saying how she met her husband Jim and answer the questions.**

1 What instrument did Jim play in the band?

2 How many members were there in the band?

3 Where did Sam work?

4 When did Sam tell Jim that she'd seen him before in his band?

2 🔊 20 **Listen again and mark the sentences T (true) or F (false).**

1 Jim's band had some local support. ☐
2 Jim always played his trumpet at the front of the stage. ☐
3 Sam tried to meet Jim when he was in a band. ☐
4 Jim left the band after a year. ☐
5 Sam was Jim's boss at the theatre. ☐
6 Sam kept her secret from Jim until they were married. ☐

GRAMMAR

3 Match the sentence halves.

1 You had better leave soon ☐
2 You're supposed to arrive before 9 am ☐
3 The test was really difficult ☐
4 There was a lot of traffic ☐
5 The more I listen to the new Kaiser Chiefs album, ☐
6 Dad says it's getting more ☐
7 Even though I didn't know anyone there, ☐
8 In spite of really studying hard, ☐

a but somehow I managed to pass.
b and we were only just able to get to the airport in time.
c and more difficult to find parking in the city centre.
d I failed the test badly.
e if you don't want to get a 'late' mark.
f I still really enjoyed the party.
g if you don't want to miss the train.
h the more I like it.

VOCABULARY

4 Complete the missing words.

1 To c_____ to the Internet you need a w_____ r_____.
2 To p_____ your laptop in you need a p_____ l_____ and an a_____ (if you're in a foreign country).
3 If you want to do video conferencing you need a w_____ and maybe a h_____.
4 To keep your phone safe you should use a p_____ c_____.
5 To connect your keyboard to your computer you might use a U_____ p_____.
6 If your laptop is out of power you will need to use the c_____.
7 If your computer is slow when you b_____ the Internet, you need to u_____ your system.
8 This software lets you s_____ your laptop and your phone so they're always up-to-date with each other.

5 Use one word from each list to complete the reported statements. There are two extra words in each list.

recommended | confessed | enquired
introduced | announced | complained

out with | engaged | in love with
up with | on a date | a family

1 'We're expecting our first baby in May.'
   She _____ that they were starting _____.

2 'You really should go to the cinema with George. You'll really like him.'
   He _____ going _____ with George.

3 'Are Sue and Mike a couple?'
   He _____ whether Sue was going _____ Mike.

4 'I can't hide my feelings any longer. I'm mad about you.'
   She _____ that she was falling _____ me.

UNITS 5 & 6

DIALOGUE

6 Put the dialogue in order.

- [ ] OLIVIA No, I'm tired of doing that. They never fix it properly. It's time for a new one.
- [ ] OLIVIA What! Today is Monday. I'm not waiting five days. I'm off to the shops. Now!
- [ ] OLIVIA Not if they don't fix it properly. It will just be a waste of my time.
- [ ] OLIVIA You always say that but then you never do.
- [ ] OLIVIA I don't know. I was trying to save a document and the whole computer crashed.
- [1] OLIVIA I don't believe it. My laptop's broken again.
- [ ] LIAM It sounds serious. You'd better take it to the repair shop.
- [ ] LIAM Well I will this time. I promise. I'll take a look at it over the weekend.
- [ ] LIAM Again? What is it this time?
- [ ] LIAM What! It will be miles cheaper to get it fixed. It's the best solution by far.
- [ ] LIAM Well at least let me have a look at it first. Maybe I can fix it.

READING

7 Read the article and put the events in order.

- [ ] He connects the hose pipe with the toilet.
- [ ] The boy is presented with a bill to pay.
- [ ] He asks the club for help.
- [ ] The boy is fishing on a lake with his friends.
- [ ] He loses his phone.
- [ ] The police question the boy about his actions.
- [ ] The club owner arrives.
- [ ] Water pours into the club.
- [ ] He arrives at the club with equipment to help him find his phone.

WRITING

8 Write a paragraph of about 120 words about an occasion when you had a problem with technology. Include:

- what the problem was
- how it affected you
- what you did to try and solve the problem

Desperate measures

The amount of time that teenagers spend in front of a screen is a huge concern for many parents all over the world. But are they worrying unnecessarily? After all, didn't their parents worry about how much time they spent in front of the TV every day? Aren't computers just the modern-day equivalent of the television or is it more than that? Many experts seem to think that many teenagers are actually addicted to technology and would find it very difficult to spend a day without it. The parents of one 16-year-old boy in Germany may have agreed with them when they found out just how far their son would go for his mobile phone.

The boy was on a fishing trip in a boat on a small lake with his friends when his phone slipped out of his hand and fell into the water – gone forever, so it would seem. But the boy refused to accept that that would be the last he would ever see of it. Even though he knew that the phone itself would be ruined, he was determined to retrieve the data card it contained with all his contact information and photos on it. This information was far too important to lose, and so he started to think what he could do to find the phone.

His first plan involved asking the fishing club, who owned the lake, if he could borrow a diving suit so he could jump into the water and search for the phone. Unsurprisingly they decided he couldn't and advised him to give up trying to find his phone. It was then he realised this was something he was going to have to do on his own when no one was watching. So later that night he went back to the lake with two water pumps and some hose pipes. His idea was simple. He was going to drain all the water out of the lake and find his phone lying at the bottom.

He decided that the best place to pump the water into would be the club's toilet. He managed to connect one end of the pipe to the pump and put the other end into the toilet. However, what he didn't know was that the toilet was connected to a small tank rather than a larger sewer system. The result was that the tank was quickly filled up and the water started to flood into the club car park. The boy tried to stop the flow but the more he tried, the worse the situation got and before he knew it there was water everywhere. When the club owner arrived he immediately called the police, leaving the boy with a lot of explaining to do. Sadly the boy was unable to find his phone. All he got was a big bill for the cost of cleaning up the mess he had created.

7 ALWAYS LOOK ON THE BRIGHT SIDE

GRAMMAR

Ways of referring to the future (review)
SB page 68

1 ★☆☆ Write sentences with the correct future form of the verbs.

0 I / play / tennis / with Milly / tomorrow
I'm playing tennis with Milly tomorrow.

1 My dad / go / to / Berlin / on business / next month
_____

2 The / lesson / start / in / ten minutes
_____

3 As soon as / Mum / get / home / we / go / to / the cinema
_____

4 We / not have dinner / until / Dad / come / home
_____

5 Tina and Tom / stay / with / their aunt / in / Mexico / in / the summer holidays
_____

2 ★★☆ Complete the dialogue with the correct form of the verbs. Use the present continuous or *going to*.

SALLY ⁰ *Are you coming* (you / come) on the school trip this summer?

NATHAN I'm not sure. I ¹_____ (ask) my parents this evening.

SALLY Matt and Lucy ²_____ (not plan) to come. They ³_____ (travel) overland to Turkey with their family this summer.

NATHAN That sounds exciting.

SALLY Yes, they ⁴_____ (drive) across France, Switzerland and Italy. Then they ⁵_____ (take) a car ferry from Italy to Turkey, via Greece.

NATHAN Awesome! When ⁶_____ (Mr Jones / hold) the meeting about the school trip?

SALLY He ⁷_____ (organise) it for next Saturday at 2 pm.

3 ★★☆ Complete the mini-dialogues with the correct future form of the verbs in brackets.

1 A What _____ (you / do) on Saturday?
  B I _____ (go) to a craft fair with my sister.

2 A Do you think your mum _____ (let) you come and stay for the weekend?
  B Yes, I think so. I _____ (ask) her tonight.

3 A What time _____ (the football match / start) on Saturday?
  B It _____ (start) at two o'clock.

4 A I _____ (look for) a Saturday job. I'd like to work in a clothes shop.
  B Really? My brother and I _____ (join) a climbing club so I can't get a Saturday job.

5 A It's my birthday tomorrow. I hope it _____ (be) sunny because we _____ (have) a barbecue in the afternoon!
  B I don't think it _____ (rain) tomorrow. The weather's been so nice today.

6 A What time _____ (the train / leave)?
  B It _____ (leave) at six o'clock.

4 ★★☆ Will it happen or won't it happen? What do you think? Read the notes and write sentences.

0 Scientists (build) a lift into space.
Scientists won't build a lift into space.

1 Your computer (have) a sense of smell.
_____

2 Facebook still (be) the biggest social network.
_____

3 Robots (do) all the work on farms.
_____

4 Planes (fly) without pilots.
_____

5 We (be able to) upload the contents of our brains to our computers.
_____

6 People (be able to) touch each other through their phones.
_____

7 ALWAYS LOOK ON THE BRIGHT SIDE

Future continuous and future perfect
SB page 69

5 ★☆☆ Write sentences in the future continuous.

The holiday's finally here. I'm so excited. This time tomorrow …

1 I / swim / in the sea

2 Sam / look for / shells on the beach

3 Mum / explore / the town

4 Dad / buy / food / at the local market

6 ★★☆ Complete the mini-dialogues with the verbs in the future perfect tense.

1 A We're late. They _____ everything by the time we get there. (eat)
   B I'm sure they _____ something for us. (leave)

2 A Hi, Miriam. I thought you were coming round to my house this afternoon. Everybody's here.
   B I am coming. I'll be there at six.
   A But everybody _____ home by then. (go)

3 A Are you looking forward to the charity swimming event tomorrow?
   B Yes. By this time tomorrow, we _____ across the Bosphorus from Asia to Europe. (swim)

4 A Have you got any plans for the future?
   B Yes. By the time I'm thirty, I _____ around the world. (travel)

7 ★★☆ Choose the correct option to complete the mini-dialogues.

1 A Dad's plane lands at eight o'clock.
   B It's 8.30 now. His plane *will be landing / will have landed*.

2 A Hey, you're going to the Lake District this weekend, right?
   B Yes, by this time on Saturday, I *will be sailing / will sail* across Lake Windermere.

3 A By the time I'm fifty, they *will be finding / will have found* a cure for cancer. I'm sure.
   B I hope so.

4 A The show starts at 7 pm.
   B Then I'm sorry, I can't come. I *will be eating / will eat* dinner with my family at that time.

5 A Mum, I'm going round to Matt's house.
   B What about your homework?
   A I *will have done / will do* it later.

8 ★★☆ Complete the email with the phrases in the list.

'll be having | 'll send | 'll have been shopping
'll be | 'll be going | 'll have seen | 'll text
'll be staying | 'll have visited

Hey Lily,

Well, this time tomorrow, I ¹_____ in London. How cool is that! We ²_____ at a hotel on the South Bank. I Googled it and it's near the Globe Theatre. I ³_____ you a photo when we get there. I know you love anything to do with the theatre and everything about Shakespeare! On the first day, we ⁴_____ to the Tower of London. My mum's keen to see the Crown Jewels. I just want to see the ravens and the Beefeaters, of course. Oh, yes! And guess what? We ⁵_____ lunch in Speedy's Sandwich Bar and Café on North Gower Street – the one that Benedict Cumberbatch always goes to in the Sherlock Holmes TV series. I can't wait.

So anyway, by the end of the trip, I ⁶_____ the London Dungeons. I ⁷_____ the view from the top of the Shard, and I ⁸_____ at Camden Market. Amazing!

I ⁹_____ you as soon as I get there.

See you soon.

Tanya

GET IT RIGHT!

will

Learners often confuse *would* and *will*.

✓ I think it **will** be a good experience.

✗ I think it ~~would~~ be a good experience.

Complete the sentences with *will* or *would*.

1 I hope the exam _____ be OK, but to be honest, I'm dreading it.

2 If Dan wasn't such a pessimist, he _____ be much more fun to be with.

3 We're about to go out so I _____ call you later.

4 Thanks for the offer. I _____ be very happy to accept.

5 Sally's really looking forward to visiting us. We _____ have a great time.

6 James is on the point of changing his job. He _____ like to spend less time commuting.

VOCABULARY

Word list

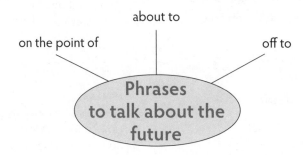

Feelings about future events

Hope for the future
have a really good feeling about
feel quite positive
be really looking forward to

Concerns for the future
dread
just not know where to start
be really worried about
get so worked up about
be a bit unsure about
have a bad feeling about
feel quite apprehensive about

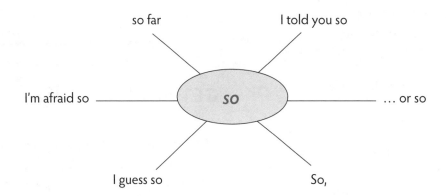

Key words in context

attitude	Kate always thinks good things will happen. She has a very positive **attitude** to life.
cheer (someone) up	My best friend always **cheers me up**. When I'm sad, she makes me feel happy again.
conscious	When he found him at the bottom of the cliff, he was still **conscious**. He could talk to us.
incapable	My friend James is **incapable** of saying anything negative about anybody. He's such a nice person.
inspirational	Steve Jobs made an **inspirational** speech at the 2005 Stanford graduation ceremony.
pessimist	Dan is a terrible **pessimist**. He always thinks something bad will happen.
quote	'All the world's a stage, and all the men and women merely players …' is a **quote** from Shakespeare's play *As You Like It*.
support	My granddad had a lot of **support** from the nurses. They really helped him to get better.
unfortunate	It was **unfortunate** that it rained at my sister's wedding.

7 ALWAYS LOOK ON THE BRIGHT SIDE

Phrases to talk about the future
SB page 68

1 ★☆☆ **Complete with one word.**

1 A Hi, Helen. I was on the p_____ of calling you.
  B Really? That's strange.
2 A I'm o_____ to the cinema. I'll see you later.
  B OK. Enjoy the film.
3 A We're a_____ to have dinner. Would you like to join us?
  B That's OK thanks. I've just eaten.

2 ★★☆ **Match the sentence halves. Then match them to the pictures.**

1 I always feel nervous when I'm about ☐
2 We are on the point of ☐
3 I'm off ☐

a to go to the dentist's.
b to the park. Would you like to come?
c finishing the experiment.

 A ☐
 B ☐

 C ☐

3 ★★★ **Write true sentences for you. Include the phrases in brackets.**

1 (about to) _____

2 (on the point of) _____

3 (off to) _____

Feelings about future events **SB page 71**

4 ★★☆ **Match the phrases (1–6) with the phrases with similar meaning (a–f).**

1 I'm feeling quite apprehensive. ☐
2 I'm dreading it. ☐
3 I've got a good feeling about it. ☐
4 I'm a bit unsure about it. ☐
5 I'm getting so worked up about it. ☐
6 I just don't know where to start. ☐

a I think it's going to be fine.
b I'm a bit nervous.
c I'm a little uncertain about it.
d I'm not looking forward to it at all.
e I'm not sure what to do first.
f It's really upsetting me.

WordWise **SB page 73**

so

5 ★★☆ **Complete the mini-dialogues with the phrases in the list.**

so far | I told you so | I'm afraid so | or so
I guess so | So

1 A You were right. Sarah will be playing in our team.
  B _____. That's great news.
2 A How many people will be coming on Saturday?
  B I'm not sure. A hundred people have bought tickets _____.
3 A _____, will you be coming to the Science Museum on Monday?
  B I don't know yet. I'll let you know as soon as I can.
4 A Will we all be wearing the same costumes for the show?
  B _____ but I'm not sure.
5 A Do I have to hand my essay in on Tuesday?
  B _____. All essays have to be in by 3 pm Tuesday. That's the final deadline.
6 A I've got to tidy my room by lunchtime.
  B I've got an hour _____ free. I'll help you.

READING

1 **REMEMBER AND CHECK** Answer the questions. Then check your answers in the blog on page 67 of the Student's Book.

1 What does Jim choose to do every day?

2 What did the doctors and nurses in the operating room think when they saw Jim?

3 What did Jim say he was allergic to?

4 What will the writer of the blog choose to find something positive about?

2 Scan the article quickly. What is the significance of each of these numbers? Write a sentence for each.

1 14
2 30
3 2,000
4 300

There is no success without failure

Think of somebody you really admire. Then read their biography. You will probably find that their success didn't come easily. Many famous artists, writers, inventors, sports people, actors and scientists overcame difficulties in their childhood. When the comedian Jim Carrey was fourteen years old, his father lost his job. Jim Carrey took a factory job in the evenings after school to help pay the family's bills.

Sometimes, their success was a surprise, even to themselves. The famous scientist Alexander Fleming said, 'When I woke up just after dawn on 28th September, 1928, I certainly didn't plan to revolutionise all medicine by discovering the world's first antibiotic, or bacteria killer. But I guess that was exactly what I did.'

Another scientist, Thomas Edison, the inventor of the light bulb, believed that every failure was a step towards success. He said, 'If I find 10,000 ways something won't work, I haven't failed. I am not discouraged, because every wrong attempt is another step forward.'

Stephen King, the American author of many horror, science fiction and fantasy books, didn't have immediate success. In fact, he was on the verge of giving up when he finally found success. His first book, *Carrie*, was rejected 30 times and he threw it into the rubbish bin (no digital copies in those days!). His wife took it out of the bin and encouraged him to send it to other publishers. Finally, it was accepted and it became a huge success. Stephen King went on to sell hundreds of millions of copies of his books.

Some people only become successful after their deaths. The artist Vincent Van Gogh only sold one painting in his lifetime and that was to a friend. Despite this, he kept painting and he painted more than 2,000 artworks in a decade. Now his paintings are very popular and they sell for millions of pounds.

Michael Jordan, the world's most famous basketball player, was rejected by his high school basketball team. He said, 'I can accept failure, everyone fails at something. But I can't accept not trying.' He went on to win the NBA's Most Valuable Player award five times.

One thing all these people have in common is determination to reach their goal no matter what. I leave you with this famous quote from Michael Jordan:

'I've missed more than 9,000 shots in my career. I've lost almost 300 games. 26 times I've been trusted to take the game-winning shot and missed. I've failed over and over and over again in my life and that is why I succeed.'

3 Read the article again. Match the questions (1–6) with the answers (a–f).

1 Who can accept failure but can't accept not trying?
2 Who woke up one morning and discovered something that went on to save millions of people's lives?
3 Who said that every failure was a step towards success?
4 Who worked after school to help buy food for his family?
5 Who only sold one piece of his work in his lifetime?
6 Whose work was rejected thirty times?

a Vincent Van Gogh
b Stephen King
c Michael Jordan
d Jim Carrey
e Alexander Fleming
f Thomas Edison

4 Find another famous author, sports person or singer who failed at first and then succeeded. Write a short paragraph about his/her failure and later success.

7 ALWAYS LOOK ON THE BRIGHT SIDE

DEVELOPING WRITING

A leaflet

1 Quickly read the leaflet and circle the answers.

1 At breakfast, Holly will …
   A play her favourite song.
   B sing her favourite song.
   C listen to her favourite song.
2 Holly will be spending the day …
   A near a lake.   B near the sea.   C up a mountain.
3 She will be watching … in the afternoon.
   A a play   B a film   C the stars
4 The day will end with her friends …
   A near a lake.   B in a castle.   C on a beach.

The Best Day of Your Life
A day designed especially for you!

9.30 am Kick off

When you come down to breakfast, your favourite upbeat 'happy' song will be playing. You will sit down to an amazing breakfast. This will include all your favourite breakfast goodies, and I mean all of them.

Breakfast menu

Cereals with strawberries, hazelnuts and chocolate
Scrambled eggs with mushrooms and toast
A big mug of creamy hot chocolate with a chocolate spoon

10.30 am Vintage Extravaganza

We will be driving to Alnwick Castle on the coast of Northumberland in your favourite sports car – a Jaguar E-type. We'll be at the castle around midday. All your friends will already have arrived.

1 pm Lunch

Lunch will be a barbecue in the castle grounds. Your favourite band, All Directions, will be playing.

2.30 pm Performance of a Lifetime

There will be an open-air performance of your favourite play in the grounds of the castle. And guess who'll be starring in it? Yes, Darcy Night Carol will play the leading role.

8 pm Star Gazing on the Beach

We will be walking to the beach to sit and watch the stars. At around 8.30 pm, we'll be toasting marshmallows on a campfire (your dad will be in charge of that) and looking for your favourite stars.

I know you're going to love it, Holly. Thanks a million for being my best friend.

2 Find synonyms to these words in the leaflet.

1 start _____
2 positive _____
3 good things _____
4 very old _____
5 outdoor _____
6 Thank you very much _____

3 Read the leaflet again and answer the questions.

1 What will Holly be drinking for breakfast?

2 How will Holly be getting to Alnwick Castle?

3 What will Holly and her friends be doing for lunch?

4 Who will be starring in the lead role of the play?

5 What will Holly and her friends be doing in the evening?

4 You are going to write a leaflet outlining 'a perfect day' for your best friend. First find out what he/she would most like to do. Write questions to ask your friend.

5 Now you are ready to plan your leaflet. Write notes for each section.

Title

Morning

Afternoon

Evening

Message to your friend

6 Write the leaflet in 200–250 words.

CHECKLIST

- The leaflet uses informal language
- The language and vocabulary is positive
- It is clear and concise
- Factual information such as times and places is clearly stated

LISTENING

1 🔊 21 Listen and write the numbers of the conversations, 1, 2 or 3 in the boxes.

  a It's about someone who wants to be in the school orchestra. ☐
  b It's about someone who wants to be in a band. ☐
  c It's about someone who wants to be in the basketball team. ☐

2 🔊 21 Listen again and mark the sentences T (true) or F (false).

CONVERSATION 1
1 Marcus will be playing in the orchestra tonight. ☐
2 May might start piano lessons. ☐

CONVERSATION 2
1 Matt has got a chance of being picked for the team because he's tall. ☐
2 Luckily nobody else wants to be in the basketball team. ☐

CONVERSATION 3
1 Jamie will not be joining the band. ☐
2 Amanda plays the drums really well. ☐

DIALOGUE

1 Put the dialogue in order.

☐	SIMON	Don't let it get you down. Your term grades are really good. You were probably just having a bad day.
1	SIMON	Hey, Miranda, cheer up! Things can't be that bad.
☐	SIMON	You see, there is light at the end of the tunnel.
5	SIMON	Hang in there, Miranda. You'll pass it next time.
☐	MIRANDA	Yes, they can. I've failed my Physics exam.
☐	MIRANDA	Thanks, you two. You've really cheered me up.
☐	HELENA	And anyway, you've just got one more year of Physics and then you can give it up.
☐	HELENA	Yes, Simon's right. Look on the bright side, Miranda. You only failed the Physics exam. You could have failed the Chemistry and Maths exams too!

Pronunciation
Intonation: encouraging someone
Go to page 120. 🔊

PHRASES FOR FLUENCY SB page 73

1 Circle the correct phrases to complete the email.

Hi Kate,

Guess what? I've entered a competition to win a trip to Iceland. My mum warned me not to ¹*go for it / get my hopes up*. Hundreds of people enter competitions like this one. But it's not like I'll ²*make a fool of myself / go for it* or anything. My dad told me to ³*go for it / get my hopes up* anyway. Someone has to win and that someone might be me. Dad's got a very positive attitude to life. ⁴*Fair enough / Anyway*, he's always been successful so he's got nothing to be negative about. But maybe his positivity is the reason for his success. ⁵*Anyway / Fair enough*, I've entered the competition and if I win, I want you to come to Iceland with me. If you don't try, you don't succeed and I've got nothing to lose ⁶*for a start / to make a fool of*.

So fingers crossed we're off to Iceland!

Love

Natalie

2 Complete these parts of the conversations with the phrases from Exercise 1.

1 MAY Are you going to tell him?
  GINA No, I don't want to be the one to tell him.
  MAY _____ . I expect Mr Williams will.

2 GINA My piano teacher's really good. You can come and practise with me.
  MAY Why not? I'll _____ .

3 MATT Do you reckon I've got a chance of being in the team? I've got myself really worked up about it.
  HARRY You shouldn't let it get you down like this. Now, I don't want to _____ , but I think you've got a chance.

4 HARRY That's tall! You should get in the team – no problem. However, I know Mike and Jake want to get in the team too.
  MATT Everyone wants to be in the basketball team and there's only one place. I don't want to _____ .

5 PIA Hey, did you hear? Jamie wants to join us.
  JOE Well, he can't, Pia.
  PIA Why not?
  JOE Well, _____ , he can't play any musical instruments.

6 JOE Maybe a few notes. _____ , I've already asked Amanda.
  PIA Asked her what?

CAMBRIDGE ENGLISH: First

Reading and Use of English part 2

1 For questions 1–8, read the text below and think of the word which best fits each gap. Use only one word in each gap. There is an example at the beginning (0).

Top tips for revising

Are you somebody **0** _who_ gets very stressed before exams? Well, a little bit of stress is a good thing **1**_____ it encourages you to work hard. However, a lot of stress is not good for you and it can cause tiredness and forgetfulness. This means you won't be at your best **2**_____ you take the exam.

Here are five tips to help you cope **3**_____ the stress. Firstly, eat healthily. Eat lots of fruit and vegetables and always have a good breakfast before you go to school. Don't eat too many sweets or too **4**_____ chocolate and don't drink cola or sugary drinks. Secondly, get **5**_____ of sleep. We recommend eight to ten hours a night. Thirdly, do some exercise. Exercise helps you **6**_____ relax and gives you more energy, **7**_____ make sure you include some in your revision timetable. Fourthly, don't leave all your revision until the night before the exam. You won't remember any of it in the morning and you'll feel very tired. Finally, after the exam, don't compare answers with your friends. You've finished the exam and so there is no point worrying about it anymore. Keep busy and enjoy life **8**_____ you wait to get the results.

Exam guide: open cloze

In this part of the test, there is a cloze text with eight gaps. You must fill the gaps with the correct words to complete the text.

- Read the whole text for general understanding. Remember to give yourself time to read the questions, skim the text, answer the questions, and then check at the end.
- The gaps usually have to be filled with some vocabulary and some grammar words such as relative pronouns, prepositions and auxiliary verbs.
- Think what kind of word is missing. Is it a preposition or is it a linking word or a verb? Look at the words that come immediately before it and after it.
- These are some common kinds of missing words:
  prepositions like *to* and *for*
  linking words like *or* and *but*
  auxiliary verbs like *was* and *will*
  relative pronouns like *that* and *who*
  question words like *what* and *where*
  time expressions like *for*, *ago* and *since*

2 For questions 1–8, read the text below and think of the word which best fits each gap. Use only one word in each gap. There is an example at the beginning (0).

It's sunny so I'm happy

Over the last few decades a lot of research has been done on the relationship **0** _between_ mood and weather.

People believe that warm sunny weather cheers people **1**_____. But is this actually true? If you read the international lists of the happiest countries in the world, places like Norway, Sweden, Canada, Denmark and Finland **2**_____ always top of the list. They are all countries that have the fewest hours of daylight and sunshine. Indeed, they are not the warmest countries **3**_____ the coldest countries. It looks **4**_____ the opposite is true.

To confirm this theory, the most northerly islands in Scotland – Shetland, Orkney and the Outer Hebrides – have **5**_____ found to be the happiest region in the whole **6**_____ the UK. How can this be? It's the coldest region and it only has around 1,000 hours of sunshine a year **7**_____ to the UK average of 1,340 hours of sunshine. Is it the weather **8**_____ is it something else that affects your mood? What do you think?

8 MAKING LISTS

GRAMMAR
Conditionals (review) SB page 76

1 ★☆☆ Match the sentence halves.

1. I'll put the coffee on — f
2. If you hadn't been late, — d
3. If my dad gets up first, — i
4. I wouldn't post that photo on Facebook — a
5. If you find the homework difficult, — h
6. You'd have passed the test — b
7. If I had the chance, — c
8. People don't usually go by boat — e
9. Hannah would be more popular — g

a. if I were you.
b. if you'd studied harder.
c. I'd go to the USA.
d. you'd have seen the beginning of the film.
e. if they can afford the air fare.
f. if I get up first.
g. if she didn't say such nasty things.
h. I'll help you.
i. he makes breakfast.

2 ★★☆ Complete the sentences from the prompts.

0. If we go to Paris, / visit / the Louvre museum.
   If we go to Paris, we'll visit the Louvre museum.

1. If Charles didn't work so much, / have / time / relax
   _____
2. Mark would have taken part in the race if / not break / leg
   _____
3. If people love cats, / often / not like / dogs much
   _____
4. Steve will buy a car if / his father / lend him / money
   _____
5. Ed would ask Jenny out if / not be / so shy
   _____
6. Anne wouldn't have fallen if / see / ice / the path
   _____

3 ★★★ Complete the gaps with the correct form of the verb given.

0. If I *had* (have) more free time, I *would go* (go) to the cinema more often.

1. If Denise _____ (come) to my party last night, she _____ (meet) my cousin.
2. Sue _____ (put) on weight if she _____ (go on) eating like this.
3. If people _____ (own) a car, they normally _____ (not use) public transport as much.
4. We _____ (visit) our grandmother more often if she _____ (live) closer.
5. If we _____ (see) Peter, we _____ (tell) him you called.
6. You _____ (not fall) off your bike last night if you _____ (not ride) so fast.
7. If James _____ (be) older, he _____ (be able) to see that film.
8. In general, an injection _____ (not hurt) so much if you _____ (relax) completely.

4 ★★★ Complete the text with the words in the list. There are two you don't need.

don't | will | can't | hadn't | won't
had | 'd have | would | had | wasn't
'd have | is | can't | wouldn't have

Steve is going to do his driving test. His instructor has given him a checklist of things to do when he takes his test. He said, 'Check the car seat. If the seat ¹_____ too far back, you ²_____ find it hard to reach the pedals. And if you ³_____ reach the pedals easily you ⁴_____ drive smoothly. Check the mirrors. If you ⁵_____ look in them, you ⁶_____ see the traffic behind or beside you.' Steve just thought, 'I think I'm going to fail. Not enough lessons. If I ⁷_____ had more time, I ⁸_____ taken more lessons.'

The test was a bit of a disaster. Afterwards he spoke to his instructor. 'If I ⁹_____ remembered to check the mirrors, I ¹⁰_____ driven out into the traffic like I did. I ¹¹_____ passed if I ¹²_____ hit that wall.'

8 MAKING LISTS

Mixed conditionals SB page 77

5 ★★☆ Write mixed conditional sentences about these situations.

0 I don't have a big car. I didn't give all my friends a lift to the match.
   If I had a big car, I'd have given all my friends a lift to the match.

1 I didn't read his text carefully. Now I don't know where to meet him.

2 Kim didn't see the step. Now she feels really silly.

3 Len arrived very early. Now he's waiting for his friends.

4 I can't help you with your Spanish homework. I didn't study Spanish at university.

5 I left the map at home. I don't know the way to their house.

6 Monica doesn't like opera. She didn't accept Oliver's invitation.

7 Tessa didn't watch the last episode. She doesn't know the ending.

8 Tim is in a hospital bed. He lost control of the car.

6 ★★★ Complete these mixed conditional sentences. Make them true for you.

1 If I had _____ last week,
   I _____ now.

2 If I hadn't _____ last night,
   I wouldn't _____ now.

3 I wouldn't _____ now if I had _____ last term.

4 I would _____ now if I had _____ last year.

Pronunciation
Weak forms with conditionals
Go to page 120.

7 ★★★ Look at the pictures and write a conditional sentence for each.

0 If mum *liked our music, she wouldn't have complained about the noise.*

1 He _____

2 They _____

3 If he _____

GET IT RIGHT!
Conditionals

Learners often use the wrong verb form in conditional clauses.

✓ *I would have remembered if I **had made** a list.*
✗ *I would have remembered if I made a list.*

The underlined parts of the sentences are incorrect. Rewrite the sentences correctly.

1 If the police <u>didn't look</u> into the matter, the crime would never have been discovered.

2 Unless we come up with some new ideas, we <u>wouldn't have</u> a chance of winning the competition.

3 Dave will get the answer as long as we <u>helped</u> him.

4 Suppose I did go to the party, what <u>will</u> I wear?

5 Provided that the calculations were correct, the structure <u>would</u> be totally safe.

6 Come to my house by eight at the latest, otherwise we <u>would</u> miss the beginning of the film.

VOCABULARY

Word list

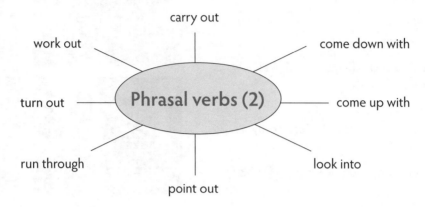

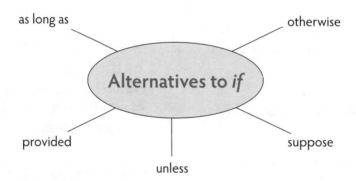

Key words in context

apparently	That café's always empty – **apparently** the food is really bad there.
calculations	It went wrong because the **calculations** were done badly.
cloth	This jacket isn't hot because it's made of a very light **cloth**.
concrete	The city wasn't beautiful – all the buildings were grey and made of **concrete**.
infection	Wash the cut on your hand right away, to avoid **infection**.
measure	The room is incredibly small – it only **measures** 1.5 metres by 3 metres.
procedure	To make a complaint, you have to fill in a form – that's the **procedure** here.
relevant	That's an interesting story, but it isn't very **relevant** to what we're talking about.
sacred	In India, people don't eat cows because they're **sacred**.
specific	Your back hurts? Please be more **specific** – your lower back or your upper back?
statement	Please answer 'Yes' or 'No' to each **statement** in the questionnaire.
structure	The new bridge is a very beautiful **structure**.

8 MAKING LISTS

Phrasal verbs (2) SB page 76

1 ★☆☆ Make a list of eight phrasal verbs from the table. You need to use one of the verbs twice.

turn	out	
come	through	
carry	up	with
look	into	
work	down	
point		
run		

1 _____
2 _____
3 _____
4 _____
5 _____
6 _____
7 _____
8 _____

2 ★★☆ Rewrite the sentences by replacing the underlined phrase with the correct form of a phrasal verb from Exercise 1.

0   The strange noises in the night <u>were discovered</u> to be the neighbour's cat.
    The strange noises in the night turned out to be the neighbour's cat.

1   I didn't know where the shop was until Kate <u>showed me</u> the store guide.

2   The instructions for the game were really long, so we just <u>looked at</u> them quickly.

3   The head teacher is <u>investigating</u> the disappearance of the school's pet snake.

4   We couldn't think of what to do until Sally <u>suddenly had</u> a brilliant idea.

5   Janet was having difficulty <u>solving</u> the clues in the crossword.

6   Some volunteers are <u>making</u> repairs to old people's houses.

7   I think we ate something bad – we all <u>got ill with</u> a stomach bug.

3 ★★★ Write a sentence for a time when you or someone you know …

1   came down with something.

2   came up with the solution for something.

3   ran through something with someone.

4   worked something out.

5   turned out to be something.

6   carried something out.

Alternatives to *if* SB page 79

4 ★★☆ Complete the sentences with one of the alternatives to *if*.

1   We need to take the first train in the morning. _____ , we'll be late.

2   _____ Mum heard you say that! She'd be really angry!

3   You can borrow my book _____ you give it back to me tomorrow.

4   Dad said I can't go on the school trip to Russia _____ I buy some travel insurance.

5   You can go there without a visa _____ you don't stay more than three months.

5 ★★★ Rewrite these sentences using alternatives to *if*. Sometimes there is more than one possibility.

1   If you didn't live here, where would you like to live?

2   The teacher said I wouldn't do well if I didn't do my homework.

3   OK, you can use my phone if you don't make long-distance calls.

4   I have to go. If I don't, I'll miss the bus.

5   Mum says we can go if we promise to be back in time for dinner.

75

READING

1 **REMEMBER AND CHECK** Circle the correct options. Then check your answers in the review on page 75 of the Student's Book.

1. A patient got a fever because the doctors didn't wear *gloves / face masks*.
2. Atul Gawande's book is called 'The Checklist Manifesto: How to *avoid accidents / get things right*.'
3. In 2001, a hospital in the US introduced a *five-point / ten-point* checklist for doctors.
4. When the same checklist was used in Michigan, infections went down by *about a half / around two-thirds*.
5. Some doctors didn't want to use Gawande's checklist because it was *too long / too difficult*.
6. Most doctors said they *would / wouldn't* want a surgeon to use the list.

2 Look at the title of the article and the photos. Read the article quickly. What do these words refer to?

well-known | eight | luxury | imagination

A famous list: Desert Island Discs

One evening in 1941, a man called Roy Plomley was sitting at home when he got an idea for a new radio programme. He wrote a letter to the BBC with his idea, and the BBC loved it. In 1942, they started to put the programme on the radio with Plomley as the presenter, and now, over seventy years later, the programme is still going strong on British radio. The name of the programme? Desert Island Discs (aka DID).

The idea of the programme is this: each week, someone well-known is invited to the programme – often an actor, a singer, a politician or someone from TV. In recent years, people like actor Colin Firth, adventurer Bear Grylls, celebrity cook Jamie Oliver and novelist J. K. Rowling have been guests. And what does the guest have to do? Well, he or she has to imagine that they have been cast away on a desert island, but that they are allowed to have eight pieces of music with them. The programme is an interview with the guest, talking about their life and work, and the eight pieces of music that the guest talks about are mixed in.

After some initial programmes, the list of eight songs was added to: guests are now also allowed to choose one book and one special, luxury item to have with them on the island. That certainly brought some cool ideas. The writer of children's books, Allan Ahlberg, asked for 'a wall to kick a football against', while famously pale-skinned singer Annie Lennox asked for suncream. And, perhaps not surprisingly, writer J. K. Rowling asked for 'an endless supply of pens and paper'.

From the very beginning, DID was incredibly popular, and it still is – there have been thousands of programmes. Plomley was the presenter for every episode until he died in 1971, and since then there have only been three other presenters. The programme's opening and closing music has never changed, and for British people it is immediately recognisable as the DID theme music.

There have been some memorable guests. One of the most controversial was an opera singer, Elizabeth Schwarzkopf, whose eight records included seven of herself singing – though, to be fair, it did seem that no one had explained the concept of the show to her well enough!

The idea of choosing just eight pieces of music to listen to forever, while you're completely alone in the world, is one that seems to capture people's imagination. What would you choose to have with you? Of course, if you like music at all, it's almost impossible to come up with a list of only eight pieces of music without leaving out things that you love. But that, perhaps, is part of the beauty of the whole DID concept.

3 Read the article again. Answer the questions.

1. How did Desert Island Discs start?
2. Who are the guests on the programme?
3. What ten things can guests take with them to the island?
4. How many presenters have there been?
5. What was different about the opera singer's choice of music?
6. What is the difficult part of making a list of eight pieces of music?

4 Imagine you could be a guest on DID. What eight pieces of music would you choose? And what would your book and your luxury item be? Write a short paragraph.

8 MAKING LISTS

DEVELOPING WRITING

Advice for travelling – an email

1 Read the emails quickly and answer the questions.

1. What is the climate of Laura's holiday destination?

2. What five items of clothing does Sean suggest taking?

3. What four essential items does he suggest taking?

Hi Sean

I live in a nice warm place but soon I'm going to travel to northern Sweden in winter, so it's going to be really cold, maybe wet too. I'm looking forward to the trip but I'm really not very sure what I should take. Can you help?

Laura

Hi Laura

That's great that you're going somewhere very different from home! But you're right, it's important to think about what to take. OK, well the first thing of course is clothes.

- Take a hat and wear it, it's the best protection against the cold. Even better if it's one that covers your ears.
- Take sweaters and coats, but it's better to think about wearing several layers of thin clothing rather than single, heavy items.
- Take at least one good pair of waterproof shoes, otherwise your feet might get cold and/or wet and that's really not what you want!
- A pair of gloves is always a good idea too, as long as they're light and waterproof.

Then, there are other essential items. Think about taking these things:

- a pair of sunglasses if you're going to be anywhere where there's snow – the bright reflection off snow can hurt unprotected eyes.
- some sunscreen. In winter? Yes – the wind can burn your skin too, so protection is good.
- lip balm to stop your lips getting sore with wind and cold.
- some simple medicines to help with colds and runny noses – always useful, especially if you're going to be a long way from a town.

So, there you go, Laura. Hope this helps and have a great holiday!

Sean

---

2 Read Sean's email again. Answer these questions.

1. What's the best kind of hat to take?

2. What's better than a single, heavy sweater?

3. What should the shoes protect you from?

4. What should gloves be like?

5. Why should you take sunglasses in winter?

6. How can you protect your lips?

7. When is it especially useful to have medicines with you?

3 Answer these questions about the email.

1. How does Sean introduce his reply?

2. How does he separate out the different things he suggests taking?

3. Each thing comes with an explanation of why Laura should take it. How does Sean indicate reasons? (There are several different ways.)

4 You're going to write an email to a friend who wants advice about what to take on holiday. Read what the friend writes. Choose a, b or c for your answer.

Hi …

I'm going on holiday to **a)** a really hot place **b)** your town/city **c)** a place you know really well. But I'm not sure what to take with me. Can you give me a nice, simple list of ideas please?
Thanks!
Jim

---

5 Write your answer. Write 150–200 words.

CHECKLIST ✓

- [ ] Start with a short introduction
- [ ] Use bullet points for your list
- [ ] Consider clothes and other things (essential items)
- [ ] For each thing, give a reason for taking it

LISTENING

1 🔊 24 Listen to Alan, Beth and Colin talking. Complete the information.

Three things I couldn't live without

Colin	Beth	Alan
1 *phone*	1 _____	1 _____
2 _____	2 _____	2 _____
3 _____	3 _____	3 _____

2 🔊 24 Listen again. Mark the statements T (true), F (false) or DS (doesn't say).

1 Their friend Jacky has gone away for a weekend with her parents. ☐
2 Jacky isn't happy that she can't take her phone. ☐
3 Colin realises he doesn't need his MP3 player if he's got his phone. ☐
4 Beth's third choice is based on the fact that she likes the colour blue. ☐
5 Alan thinks it's sad if you can only think of three things you can't live without. ☐
6 Beth doesn't like serious discussions. ☐
7 Alan doesn't accept Colin's first idea for his third thing. ☐
8 Colin considers himself to be a good guitar player. ☐

3 Write your list of three things that you couldn't live without, and why.

1 _____
2 _____
3 _____

DIALOGUE

1 Put the dialogues into the correct order.

1

☐ ADAM — Like the way that guy last night did? I think if I was a contestant on that programme, I'd have shouted at him.

☐ ADAM — But do you think you would behave better? I mean, in a situation like that.

[1] ADAM — Are you watching that reality show about people stuck on an island?

☐ ADAM — He certainly will. Well, unless one of the other people starts behaving even worse.

☐ BRIONY — Good question. And you know, I think I'd be OK, as long as the other people didn't make me angry.

☐ BRIONY — Yes, I think it's great. I love watching people behaving badly!

☐ BRIONY — And that's always a possibility, right? Listen, why don't we watch the next episode together?

☐ BRIONY — Me too. He was awful. If he carries on like that, he'll be voted off next week.

2

☐ ANGIE — Of course I will, don't worry. Why wouldn't I look after it?

☐ ANGIE — Not true. I looked after it. I just gave it back later than I'd promised.

[1] ANGIE — Can I borrow your tablet?

☐ ANGIE — Of course I would have. But OK, don't lend me the tablet. I don't mind.

☐ BRENDAN — No, it's OK. You can borrow it. Otherwise you'll never talk to me again. Just joking, Angie!

☐ BRENDAN — Why? Well, I remember you didn't really look after the camera I lent you.

☐ BRENDAN — Well, yes, I suppose so – as long as you promise to look after it.

☐ BRENDAN — Right. And if I hadn't reminded you, you'd never have given it back.

2 Choose one of the two scenarios. Write a 6–8 line dialogue between the two people.

1 Elena wants Amy to go shopping with her. Amy remembers previous shopping experiences with Elena, that weren't very good. But in the end, Amy agrees.

2 Chris wants to go and see a concert. But Chris's parents will only let Chris go if a friend goes too. Sammy doesn't really like the music in the concert.

CAMBRIDGE ENGLISH: First

Speaking part 2

1 Look at this pair of photos. How do you think the people feel in each photo?

2 🔊25 You are going to listen to Alexander talking about the photo (you will also hear an examiner). Here are some things Alexander says. Which photo is each phrase about? Write A or B in the boxes. Then listen and check.

1 It doesn't look like they're enjoying it very much. ☐
2 Apparently they've been shopping. ☐
3 It looks as though they're enjoying the nice weather. ☐
4 I don't know exactly where it is but it could be Sweden or Denmark. ☐
5 I don't think they are really very happy. ☐
6 They seem to be having a good time. ☐

3 In each of the sentences 1–6 in Exercise 2, Alexander softens what he says. For example, he doesn't say 'They have been shopping' – he says 'Apparently they've been shopping.'

How does he soften his statements in the other five sentences?

Exam guide: individual 'long turn'

In Part 2 of the First speaking exam, there will be two examiners and two candidates in the room. You will be given two pairs of photos. You will be asked to talk about one of the pairs. You have to talk about them for about a minute. The examiner will tell you what to talk about concerning the two photos.

The examiner will say, for example:
X, I'd like you to look at your two photos and compare them.
Say what you think the people feel about being outside in these situations.

- You only have one minute so try to keep talking, stopping as little as possible.
- Try to use as wide a range of vocabulary as you can.
- Make sure that you do what you're asked to do – here, for example, don't describe the photos but talk about what you think the people are feeling and why.
- Speak clearly and as confidently as you can – confidence always helps!

4 🔊25 Listen again. How well did he do? Grade his performance.

Give him 1 star for 'could do better', 2 stars for 'good' and 3 stars for 'excellent'.

1 His voice is clear. ★ ★★ ★★★
2 His word and sentence stress are good. ★ ★★ ★★★
3 He talks fluently. ★ ★★ ★★★
4 He uses a good range of vocabulary. ★ ★★ ★★★
5 He sounds natural. ★ ★★ ★★★

5 Imagine you are an exam candidate yourself. Do the same task that Alexander did and ask a friend to listen to you and grade your performance.

CONSOLIDATION

LISTENING

1 🔊 26 Listen to Dave and Maggie. Tick the things that Maggie is taking with her on holiday.

A ☐ B ☐ C ☐ D ☐ E ☐ F ☐

2 🔊 26 Listen again. Answer the questions.

1 What negative things does Maggie talk about with regard to camping?

2 Why are tablets for stomach ache on her list?

3 Why does Dave agree that it's a good idea for Maggie to take medicines with her?

4 What condition did Maggie's parents state for her taking her tablet with her?

5 What does Dave say that makes Maggie panic?

6 What does Dave say about the next time they see each other?

GRAMMAR

3 Circle the correct options.

1 I'm going to have a shower as soon as I *get / will get* home.
2 If I spoke another language as well as you do, I*'d be / was* really pleased with myself.
3 If you *don't / won't* help me, I'll be really angry with you.
4 By the time you read this, I *will have arrived / will have been arriving* in the USA.
5 I can't see you tomorrow night – we *go / are going* to my uncle's birthday party.
6 If you'd told us where you were going, we *wouldn't be / wouldn't have been* so upset now.
7 This time tomorrow, we'll *watch / be watching* my sister's first appearance on TV.
8 By next year we *will live / will have lived* in this flat for more than ten years.

VOCABULARY

4 Match the sentence halves.

1 Our weekend was ruined when my mum came ☐
2 I've got a really good feeling ☐
3 She's decided she wants to carry ☐
4 Everything will be fine unless ☐
5 We weren't sure what to do, but Sue came ☐
6 We'd better go now, otherwise ☐
7 It isn't easy to work ☐
8 Let's just take a moment, please, and run ☐

a up with a brilliant idea.
b we get home really late.
c down with a really bad cold.
d about the game tonight.
e through the names again.
f out the research, no matter what.
g we'll be late getting home.
h out why that happened.

5 Complete the words.

1 Can I just p_____ out that this isn't your first mistake.
2 We're all looking f_____ to seeing you again.
3 I hate camping, so I'm really d_____ this weekend!
4 I don't care what you do, p_____ you don't get me into trouble.
5 It's not a big problem, so why are you getting so w_____ up about it?
6 I'm not sure about our new house, but my parents feel quite p_____ about moving there.
7 We got to the address on time, but it t_____ out to be the wrong place.
8 I guess it'll be OK, but I have to say I'm a bit a_____ about tomorrow's test.

UNITS 7 & 8

DIALOGUE

6 Complete the dialogue with the phrases in the list. There are three you won't use.

so far | I'm afraid so | Anyway | for a start
cheer up | get my hopes up | go for it
Fair enough | I think so

PAUL So what happened at your interview? Oh, you look pretty unhappy. Did it go badly?

ANNIE ¹_____. In fact, almost everything went wrong. I was late ²_____.

PAUL Oh dear. Were they angry about that?

ANNIE ³_____. Well, they certainly didn't smile much. And the woman who was the main interviewer said they could only give me 15 minutes.

PAUL ⁴_____, I suppose.

ANNIE Yes, you're right. After all, they have other things to do. ⁵_____, they asked me some questions but I don't think I answered them especially well.

PAUL Well, ⁶_____. If you don't get the job, you can try other places.

ANNIE But there aren't any other places! Oh well, I'll just have to wait until they contact me, I suppose.

READING

7 Read the article and answer the questions.

Who …

0 was turned down by several record companies?
   The Beatles
1 once had a job driving trucks? _____
2 was an influence on other people in his field? _____
3 was famous for E.T. (among other things)? _____
4 was sometimes called by another name? _____
5 was turned down for a job by a famous film maker? _____
6 ended up with an art gallery showing his work? _____
7 has won Hollywood awards? _____

WRITING

8 Choose one of the people in the article. Write a dialogue of 8–10 lines between that person and a person who said 'No' to them.

Your dialogue can be either:
- at the time the person said 'No', OR
- after the rejected person became famous.

Being rejected

A lot of people who became incredibly successful had to get past a lot of rejection. Very famously, The Beatles went to several record companies before they finally found one that was willing to record one of their songs. (Imagine how the other companies felt a few years later!) But they weren't alone. Here's a short list of rejections.

Steven Spielberg, the wealthiest film director in Hollywood and a man who has won two Oscars for Best Director, tried three times as a young man to get into the University of Southern California School of Theater, Film and Television – and three times, they said 'No'. So he went somewhere else, but didn't like it much and dropped out. Thirty-five years later, and after establishing his hugely successful career, he went back and finished his degree. Imagine – if he hadn't dropped out, he wouldn't have made films like E.T.

Claude Monet is recognised now as one of the great Impressionist painters. But he was laughed at by the other painters in the Paris Salon, which was a kind of club for painters and writers who met to discuss their ideas and their work. They refused to let him join them. Little did they know that Monet would become a huge influence on other artists, and would become extremely famous in his own lifetime. There is also now a gallery in Paris called l'Orangerie that displays some of his most famous paintings and which is visited by thousands of people every year.

Charles Schultz – do you know that name? Maybe not, but you probably know the 'Peanuts' cartoons that he invented and drew for decades before he died in 2000, and which have been published in various languages all over the world. He started doing cartoons in high school, but the school wouldn't publish them in their annual end-of-year celebration book. Even Walt Disney turned him down for a job before he started his cartoon career.

In 1954, **Elvis Presley** played for just one night at a famous concert hall in Nashville. The manager fired him immediately afterwards and told him to 'go back to driving a truck'. Presley, of course, went on to become the most famous singer in the world for many years – his nickname was 'The King' and he sold millions of records and made several films too.

So, it takes persistence to make it, no matter how good you are! As our examples here show, even if you get turned down several times, you can still make it as long as you have determination and self-belief.

PRONUNCIATION

UNIT 5
The schwa sound

1 Complete the text with the words *to, and, of, for, or, a* or *an*.

0 Thank you _for_ calling David's telephone service.
1 This is _____ recorded message.
2 There are no operators free to take your call at _____ moment.
3 Press 1 _____ leave a message.
4 Press 2 if you wish to speak to _____ operator.
5 Please don't shout _____ scream at the operators.
6 Now please hang up _____ make yourself a cup _____ tea.

2 ◉16 Listen, check and repeat.

3 Circle the other unstressed words in each sentence which have little meaning and which have the schwa /ə/ sound.

UNIT 6
Linking words with /dʒ/ and /tʃ/

1 Complete the sentences with the words in the list. Circle the words linked with the /dʒ/ sound and underline the words linked with a /tʃ/ sound.

~~should~~ | can't | could | did | do
don't | just | won't | would

0 There's an extra blanket, (should you) need it.
1 You come from Australia, _____ you?
2 How _____ you learn to paint so well?
3 _____ you like a cup of tea and a biscuit?
4 _____ you know how to do a Sudoku?
5 _____ you move out of the way, please? I can't see the TV.
6 You must be tired after your long walk. _____ you sit down?
7 I haven't told anyone my secret – _____ you.
8 You can swim, _____ you?

2 ◉19 Listen, check and repeat.

PRONUNCIATION

UNIT 7
Intonation: encouraging someone

1. 🔊 22 Listen to the sentences, paying particular attention to the underlined phrases. Does the speaker sound interested (I) or uninterested (U)? Write I or U in the box next to each sentence.

   0 Don't <u>let it get you down</u>. People fail their driving test all the time. [U]
   1 Try to <u>look on the bright side</u> – if it's raining we can stay in and watch TV. [ ]
   2 I know <u>you can do it</u>. You just need a few more lessons. [ ]
   3 <u>Don't worry</u> – everything will be fine in the end. [ ]
   4 <u>Cheer up</u>. Things will seem better after a good night's sleep. [ ]
   5 <u>Hang in there</u>. Your exams will be over soon. [ ]
   6 <u>It's not the end of the world</u> – and we've got a day off next week. [ ]

2. Repeat the sentences trying to sound interested in all of them.

UNIT 8
Weak forms with conditionals

would have

1. Circle the contractions *could've*, *should've* and *would've* where they're pronounced *coulda* /ˈkʊdə/, *shoulda* /ˈʃʊdə/ and *woulda* /ˈwʊdə/ without the /v/ sound.

   0 I (would've) come if I'd known Kylie was going to be there.
   1 You should've seen the waves at the beach yesterday – they were enormous!
   2 Sarah could've passed the test but she didn't study for it.
   3 Marley would've asked you to help him if he'd known you were free.
   4 We didn't know Jack was in hospital – we would've sent a card if we'd known.
   5 I should've eaten breakfast – I'm really hungry now!
   6 The accident would've been much worse if they'd been driving faster.
   7 You could've told me – you knew it was Dad's birthday yesterday!

   > **Remember:** You don't have to say the contractions this way – but hearing them will help you understand native speakers better.

2. 🔊 23 Listen, check and repeat.

GRAMMAR REFERENCE

UNIT 5

Obligation, permission and prohibition (review)

1 We can talk about obligation and necessity by using *must*, *have to* and *(be) supposed to*.

   You **must** get there before eight o'clock. (= This is an obligation imposed by the speaker.)
   We **have to** finish our projects by Friday. (= This is an obligation imposed by someone else.)
   We'**re supposed to** switch off our phones in lessons. (= This is the rule, but we don't always follow it.)

2 We can talk about no obligation or no necessity by using *don't have to* and *don't need to*.

   You **don't have to** eat this if you don't want to.
   We **didn't need to** buy tickets – my dad gave us some.

3 We can say something is (or isn't) a good idea by using *should(n't)*.

   You **should** leave now if you don't want to miss your bus.
   I **shouldn't** eat any more or I'll feel sick.

4 We can talk about permission using *let* or *be allowed to*. *Let* is active voice, while *be allowed to* is passive voice.

   The school **lets** us use the tennis courts at the weekend.
   We're **allowed to** use the tennis courts at the weekend.

5 We can talk about prohibition using *(not) be allowed to* or *don't/doesn't let*. When we don't know, or don't want to say who it is that prohibits something, we use 'they'.

   Cyclists **are not allowed to** leave their bikes here.
   They don't let cyclists leave their bikes here.

Necessity: (didn't) need to / needn't have

We use *didn't need to* and *needn't have* to talk about the past necessity of actions. There is a small but important difference between the structures.

1 *didn't need to* usually suggests that we didn't do something because it wasn't necessary.

   I **didn't need to** go to the doctor. (I didn't go.)

2 *needn't have* means that we did something but actually it wasn't necessary.

   We **needn't have** cooked all this food – only four people turned up at the party. (We cooked a lot of food but it wasn't necessary.)

Ability in the past: could, was/were able to, managed to, succeeded in doing

1 When we talk about ability in the past, we can use *could/couldn't*, *managed to*, *was/were able to* or *succeeded (in doing)*. However, there are differences between them.

2 We use *could / couldn't* to talk about general ability in the past.

   My brother **couldn't ride** a bike until he was twelve.
   I **could do** maths in my head when I was a kid.

3 When we want to talk about no ability on a specific occasion in the past, we have three possibilities:

   I listened, but I **couldn't hear** anything.
   I worked hard, but I **didn't manage to finish** everything.
   I hurt my leg and I **wasn't able to walk** for two weeks.

4 But, when we want to talk about ability on a specific occasion in the past, we don't use *could*:

   The wall was very high but we **managed to climb** over it. (NOT: we ~~could climb~~ over it.)
   Because we bought our tickets a long time in advance, we **were able to get** them quite cheaply. (NOT: we ~~could get~~ them …)

5 We use *succeeded (in doing)* to emphasise that something was difficult in the past but we were able to do it.

   I had to wait for hours, but I **succeeded in getting** tickets.

UNIT 6

Comparatives

1 We can intensify a comparison (make it stronger) using *a lot / far / much* + comparative adjective.

   Use a calculator – it's **far easier** that way.
   Let's take a taxi, it's **much quicker**.
   It's **a lot more difficult** than I thought.

2. Comparisons with *as … as* can be made stronger with *not nearly* or *nowhere near*.
   He's **not nearly as clever as** his sister. (His sister is much cleverer than him.)
   The film is **nowhere near as good as** the book. (The book is far better than the film.)

3. We can use *just* with *as … as* to emphasise how similar two things are.
   Our team is **just as good as** yours. (The two teams are really equally good.)

4. We can use comparative *and* comparative with short adjectives or *more and more* + adjective with longer adjectives to show how comparisons become stronger over time.
   My little sister's getting **bigger and bigger** every day.
   Train tickets are getting **more and more expensive**.

5. We can use *the* + comparative (+ clause), *the* + comparative (+ clause) with short adjectives, or *the more …* adjective (+ clause), *the more …* adjective (+ clause) with longer adjectives, to show how two events affect each other.
   The longer I sat there, **the more uncomfortable** I became.
   The older people are, **the more interesting** they are.

Linkers of contrast

1. The linkers *although* and *even though* are followed by a clause. They can be used at the beginning of a sentence, or before the second clause.
   I passed my driving test, **although / even though** I made some mistakes.
   Although / Even though I made some mistakes in my driving test, I passed.

2. The linkers *despite* and *in spite of* are followed by a noun phrase or a gerund. They can be used at the beginning of a sentence, or before the second clause.
   I passed my driving test, **despite / in spite of** (making) some mistakes.
   Despite (making) some mistakes in my driving test, I passed.

3. The linkers *however* and *nevertheless* come at the beginning of a sentence and introduce a contrast with what was said in the previous sentence.
   I made some mistakes in my driving test. **However / Nevertheless**, I passed.

UNIT 7
Ways of referring to the future (review)

Some common ways to refer to the future include:

1. *be going to* for plans, intentions and evidence-based predictions
   I'm going to visit my grandparents tomorrow.

2. *will* for future facts, spontaneous decisions and offers, and feeling-based predictions
   Technology **will develop** a lot in the next twenty years.

3. the present continuous for arrangements
   We**'re taking** our cat to the vet this afternoon.

4. the present simple for events that are part of a timetable, and after time expressions like *when, before, after, until*, and *as soon as*
   I'll meet you when you **arrive** tomorrow.

Future continuous and future perfect

1. The future continuous is formed by *will* + *be* + *-ing* form of the verb.

2. We use the future continuous tense to talk about an action that will be in progress at a specified future time.
   When I'm 25, **I'll be living** in another country.

3. The future perfect tense is formed by *will* + *have* + the past participle of the verb.

4. We use the future perfect tense to talk about an action that we think will be completed by a specified future time.
   By 2025, the population **will have grown** enormously.

UNIT 8
Conditionals (review)

1. We use the zero conditional to talk about a condition and its consequence that are always true.
   If I **go** running, I always **feel** better.

2. We use the first conditional to talk about a condition and its possible future consequence.
   If you **make** a list, you**'ll remember** what you need.

3. We use the second conditional to talk about a hypothetical situation in the present.
   If I **had** more time, **I'd take up** the guitar.

4   We use the third conditional to talk about an imaginary situation in the past and its consequence in the past which is impossible to change.

*If we **had left** earlier, we **wouldn't have been** late.*

Mixed conditionals

Conditional sentences don't always follow the four patterns described above. It's possible to mix second and third conditionals.

1   If we want to talk about an imaginary / unreal past action and its present consequence, then the *if* clause follows the pattern of a third conditional and the consequence clause follows the pattern of a second conditional.

*If I**'d paid** more attention in class, I**'d know** how to do this exercise. (I didn't pay attention. I don't know how to do this exercise.)*

2   If we want to talk about how a hypothetical or imaginary present could or would change the past, then the *if* clause follows the pattern of a second conditional and the consequence clause follows the pattern of a third conditional.

*If I **had** more self-confidence, I **would have gone** and talked to him. (I didn't go and talk to him, because I don't have much self-confidence.)*

IRREGULAR VERBS

Base form	Past simple	Past participle
be	was / were	been
bear	bore	borne
beat	beat	beaten
become	became	become
begin	began	begun
bend	bent	bent
bet	bet	bet
bite	bit	bitten
blow	blew	blown
break	broke	broken
breed	bred	bred
bring	brought	brought
broadcast	broadcast	broadcast
build	built	built
burn	burned / burnt	burned / burnt
buy	bought	bought
can	could	–
catch	caught	caught
choose	chose	chosen
come	came	come
cost	cost	cost
cut	cut	cut
deal	dealt	dealt
dive	dived	dived
do	did	done
draw	drew	drawn
dream	dreamed / dreamt	dreamed / dreamt
drink	drank	drunk
drive	drove	driven
eat	ate	eaten
fall	fell	fallen
feed	fed	fed
feel	felt	felt
fight	fought	fought
find	found	found
flee	fled	fled
fly	flew	flown
forbid	forbade	forbidden
forget	forgot	forgotten
forgive	forgave	forgiven
freeze	froze	frozen
get	got	got
give	gave	given
go	went	gone
grow	grew	grown
hang	hung	hung
have	had	had
hear	heard	heard
hide	hid	hidden
hit	hit	hit
hold	held	held
hurt	hurt	hurt
keep	kept	kept
know	knew	known
lay	laid	laid
lead	led	led
learn	learned / learnt	learned / learnt
leave	left	left
lend	lent	lent
let	let	let
lie	lay	lain
light	lit	lit
lose	lost	lost
make	made	made
mean	meant	meant
meet	met	met
misunderstand	misunderstood	misunderstood
overcome	overcame	overcome
pay	paid	paid
put	put	put
quit	quit	quit
read /riːd/	read /red/	read /red/
ride	rode	ridden
ring	rang	rung
rise	rose	risen
run	ran	run
say	said	said
see	saw	seen
seek	sought	sought
sell	sold	sold
send	sent	sent
set	set	set
shake	shook	shaken
shine	shone	shone
shoot	shot	shot
show	showed	shown
shut	shut	shut
sing	sang	sung
sink	sank	sunk
sit	sat	sat
sleep	slept	slept
speak	spoke	spoken
speed	sped	sped
spend	spent	spent
spill	spilled / spilt	spilled / spilt
split	split	split
spread	spread	spread
stand	stood	stood
steal	stole	stolen
stick	stuck	stuck
strike	struck	struck
swear	swore	sworn
sweep	swept	swept
swim	swam	swum
swing	swung	swung
take	took	taken
teach	taught	taught
tear	tore	torn
tell	told	told
think	thought	thought
throw	threw	thrown
understand	understood	understood
wake	woke	woken
wear	wore	worn
win	won	won
write	wrote	written

Acknowledgements

The authors and publishers acknowledge the following sources of copyright material and are grateful for the permissions granted. While every effort has been made, it has not always been possible to identify the sources of all the material used, or to trace all copyright holders. If any omissions are brought to our notice, we will be happy to include the appropriate acknowledgements on reprinting and in the next update to the digital edition, as applicable.

The Independent for the text on p. 58 adapted from 'Mugging victim Alan Barnes plans to move house after donations reach £200,000', The Independent 02.02.2015. Copyright © The Independent;

Northern and Shell Media Publications for the text on p. 58 adapted from 'Dozens of police and firefighters surprise autistic boy after classmates all miss party' by Sarah Ann Harris. Copyright © Northern and Shell Media Publications. Reproduced by kind permission;

Text on p. 63 adapted from 'Boy drops phone on fishing trip, drains entire pond to find it' by Valerie Loftus, TheJournal.ie, 03.08.2014.

Corpus
Development of this publication has made use of the Cambridge English Corpus (CEC). The CEC is a computer database of contemporary spoken and written English, which currently stands at over one billion words. It includes British English, American English and other varieties of English. It also includes the Cambridge Learner Corpus, developed in collaboration with Cambridge English Language Assessment. Cambridge University Press has built up the CEC to provide evidence about language use that helps to produce better language teaching materials.

English Profile
This product is informed by the English Vocabulary Profile, built as part of English Profile, a collaborative programme designed to enhance the learning, teaching and assessment of English worldwide. Its main funding partners are Cambridge University Press and Cambridge English Language Assessment and its aim is to create a 'profile' for English linked to the Common European Framework of Reference for Languages (CEF). English Profile outcomes, such as the English Vocabulary Profile, will provide detailed information about the language that learners can be expected to demonstrate at each CEF level, offering a clear benchmark for learners' proficiency. For more information, please visit www.englishprofile.org

Cambridge Dictionaries
Cambridge dictionaries are the world's most widely used dictionaries for learners of English. The dictionaries are available in print and online at dictionary.cambridge.org. Copyright © Cambridge University Press, reproduced with permission.

The publishers are grateful to the following for permission to reproduce copyright photographs and material:

T = Top, B = Below, L = Left, R = Right, C = Centre, B/G = Background

p. 49 (a): ©anaken2012/Shutterstock; p. 49 (b): ©Nikita Rogul/Shutterstock; p. 49 (c): ©Pavel Kubarkov/Shutterstock; p. 49 (d): ©KonstantinChristian/Shutterstock; p. 49 (e): ©Vladimir Mucibabic/Shutterstock; p. 49 (f): ©Olga Popova/Shutterstock; p. 55: ©Edyta Pawlowska/Shutterstock; p. 57: ©Kevin Moore/Alamy Stock Photo; p. 58: ©Ian Forsyth/Getty Images; p. 59 (T): ©Goodluz/Shutterstock; p. 59 (B): ©Ann Summa/Corbis; p. 68 (T): ©NEW LINE/DARK HORSE/THE KOBAL COLLECTION; p. 68 (C): ©De Agostini Picture Library/Getty Images; p. 68 (B): ©ZORAN BOZICEVIC/AFP/Getty Images; p. 76 (L): ©Graham Wood/Associated Newspapers/REX Shutterstock; p. 76 (R): ©Sam Camp/iStock/Getty Images Plus/Getty Images; p. 77: ©Latitudestock/Gallo Images/Getty Images; p. 78: ©Kali Nine LLC/E+/Getty Images; p. 79 (L): ©Peter Phipp/Travelshots.com/Alamy Stock Photo; p. 79 (R): ©Realimage/Alamy Stock Photo; p. 80 (a): ©Paul Orr/Shutterstock; p. 80 (b): ©Natalia Siverina/Shutterstock; p. 80 (c): ©BranislavP/Shutterstock; p. 80 (d): ©Skoda/Shutterstock; p. 80 (e): ©Radu Razvan/Shutterstock; p. 80 (f): ©Don Pablo/Shutterstock.

Cover photographs by: (TL): ©Stephen Moore/Digital Vision Vectors/Getty Images; (BL): ©Pete Starman/Stone/Getty Images; (C): ©imagedb.com/Shutterstock; (TR): ©Stephen Moore/Digital Vision Vectors/Getty Images; (BR): ©Kimberley Coole/Lonely Planet Images/Getty Images.

The publishers are grateful to the following illustrators:
David Semple 60, 73
Julian Mosedale 50, 67

The publishers are grateful to the following contributors:
Blooberry: text design and layouts; Hilary Fletcher: picture research; Leon Chambers: audio recordings; Karen Elliott: Pronunciation sections; Rebecca Raynes: Get it right! exercises